Olympic Peninsula Rivers Guide

Steve Probasco

Ecopress

Corvallis, Oregon

Ecopress

POB 2004, Corvallis, Oregon 97339
Tel: 1-800-326-9272
Email: ecopress@peak.org
WWW: www.ecopress.com

Copyright © 1999

Every effort was made to make this book as accurate and up-to date as possible. However, there are no warranties, expressed or implied, that the information is suitable to any particular purpose. The maps are to suggest river structure and are not to be used for navigation. The author and publisher assume no responsibility for activities in the river corridor.

Printed in the U.S.A. on 30% post-consumer recycled paper with soy-based ink.

Library of Congress Cataloging-in-Publication Data

Probasco, Steve.
  The Olympic Peninsula Rivers Guide / Steve Probasco
      p.   cm.
  Includes bibliographical references and index.
  ISBN 0-9639705-5-0
  1.   Outdoor recreation—Washington(State)—Olympic Peninsula—Guidebooks. 2. Rivers—Washington(State)—Olympic Peninsula—Recreational use—Guidebooks. 3. Olympic Peninsula (Wash.)—Guidebooks. l. Title

GV191.42.W2 P76 1999   99-043817

10 9 8 7 6 5 4 3 2 1

Dedicated to the memory of Cecil Probasco, my dad, who taught me early in life to love the outdoors.

Olympic Peninsula Rivers

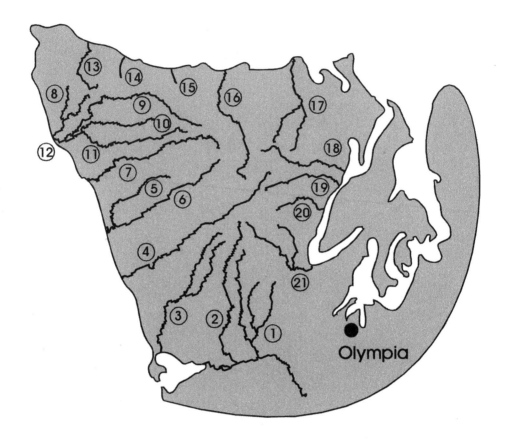

1) Satsop River - page 21
2) Wynoochee River - page 21
3) Humptulips River - page 25
4) Quinault River - page 31
5) Clearwater River - page 41
6) Queets River - page 43
7) Hoh River - page 55
8) Dickey River - page 63
9) Sol Duc River - page 65
10) Calawah River - page 81
11) Bogachiel River - page 85

12) Quillayute River - page 91
13) Hoko River - page 97
14) Pysht River - page 99
15) Lyre River - page 101
16) Elwha River - page 103
17) Dungeness - page 113
18) Dosewallips River - page 117
19) Duckabush River - page 121
20) Hamma Hamma River - page 125
21) Skokomish River - page 127

Table of Contents - Olympic Peninsula Rivers Guide

The Olympic Peninsula   9

Part I – Pacific Ocean Streams

Wynoochee River   15

Satsop River   21

Humptulips River   25

Quinault River   31

Clearwater River   41

Queets River   43

Hoh River   55

Dickey River   63

Sol Duc River   65

Calawah River   81

Bogachiel River   85

Quillayute River   91

Part II – Strait of Juan de Fuca Streams

Hoko River   97

Pysht River   99

Lyre River   101

Elwha River   103

Dungeness River   113

Part III – Hood Canal / Puget Sound Streams

Dosewallips River   117

Duckabush River   121

Hamma Hamma River   125

Skokomish River   127

The High Country   133

Final Thoughts   135

Bibliography   136

Index   137

Beaver Falls.

The Olympic Peninsula

The Beginning

Sixty million years ago, the area that is now the Olympic Peninsula lay beneath the sea. When the oceanic plates collided with the continental plates, the upheaval created, in a round-about way, the Olympic Mountains.

Erosion has, over the millennia, sculpted the upheaval. Two million years ago, during the last Ice Age, much of the Olympic Mountains we see today were carved by giant flows of ice. At least six times during the last ice age the Cordilleran ice sheet flowed across the area from the north. This gigantic glacier split as it reached the mountains, one branch heading west towards the sea and gouging out what is now the Strait of Juan de Fuca, the other traveling down the east side of the mountains forming Puget Sound.

Roughly 13,000 years ago there was a warming trend. Most of the alpine glaciers retreated before the thick continental ice sheet could melt, gouging and carving the river valleys leading from the mountains and leaving giant lakes. Granite, and other rocks foreign to the Olympics, were carried by huge icebergs and deposited high in the mountains where they can be found today.

With the exception of glaciers found high on Mt. Olympus, the glaciers seen today in the Olympics are relatively new. These formations are roughly 2,500 years old and reached their peak only two centuries ago.

From the glacial-carved valleys of the Olympics flow 11 major rivers, constantly fed by glacial melt and the seemingly incessant rains.

First Explorers

Prior to the white man's arrival, natives of the Olympic Peninsula lived in balance with their surroundings for many centuries. As in most areas of North America, the arrival of white men was the beginning of the end of the native lifestyle.

It is believed that Juan de Fuca was the first European to come ashore on the Olympic Peninsula. He was actually a Greek named Apostolos Valerianos who called himself "Juan de Fuca" while in service of the Spanish. He sailed along the western coastline of the United States in search of the fabled "Northwest Passage" between the Atlantic and Pacific Oceans. He claimed to have found it at the strait that now bears his name. It was, of course, not true, but explorers continued to look for the passage until Lewis and Clark mapped the area many years later.

In 1774, Juan Perez sailed along the coast and there is documented evidence of the European arrival. Then British, Spanish and American explorers visited the peninsula. Both Robert Gray (an American) and George Vancouver (an Englishmen) explored the coast, claiming the land for their respective countries.

In 1885, the interior of the Olympic Peninsula was explored by Lt. Joseph P. O'Neil. A few years later, an expedition led by James Cristie made a north-south crossing of the peninsula. Lt. O'Neil also returned to make and east-west crossing.

Olympic National Park

President Grover Cleveland created the Olympic Forest Reserve in 1897 to prevent the forests of the Olympic Peninsula from destruction due to poor logging practices. Ahh, such foresight so long ago! Then, in 1909, President Theodore Roosevelt proclaimed part of the reserve as a national monument. In 1938, President Franklin D. Roosevelt signed a bill establishing Olympic National Park.

The area within the park's boundary varies from sea coast, to rain forest, to sub-alpine and alpine regions. There are 57 miles of Pacific Ocean coastline within the park's boundaries, although a strip of state and private land separates the main body of the park from the coast. There are only a few roads leading into the park, so most of the travel is done on foot on over 600 miles of trails. Alternatively, floating one of the several river systems is a great way to see the park.

In the heart of the park rise the Olympic Mountains. Although not particularly high, they rise from sea level and look much taller than they really are. At 7,965 feet, Mt. Olympus is the highest peak.

The Temperate Rain Forest

The rain forest valleys on the west side of the Olympic mountains are nothing short of spectacular. The three main valleys (Hoh, Queets and Quinault) average around 12 feet of annual precipitation. Conifers can also extract the equivalent of another 30 inches of moisture from the air, as thick fogs from the ocean are frequent. This abundance of rain, combined with the mild climate creates a magnificent forest community of every imaginable shade of green.

Plant life flourishes. Maidenhair fern, oxalis, trillium, huckleberry, blackberry, salmonberry, devils club and vine maple are but a few of the more common plants. Epiphytes, plants that use trees or other structures for support, are common here. Clubmoss hangs from tree limbs, especially on the big-leaf maple trees. Licorice ferns and other epiphytes (over 130 species) thrive. These temperate rain forests host more biological matter per area than any other ecosystem in the world.

Some of the largest trees in the world are found in the rain forests of the Olympic Mountains. Sitka spruce, western hemlock, redcedar, bigleaf maple, Douglas fir and red alder are all found here. There are several specimens in this area that are the largest known for their species. These "record trees" are up to 700 years old and soar 200 feet high, adding to the magnificence of the rain forest.

Because seedlings have a hard time getting started on the thickly vegetated forest floor, they often take root on "nurse logs," which are fallen, slowly decaying trees. The roots of the new trees find their way to the ground and, after the nurse log completely rots away, it appears that these new trees are growing on stilts. It is common for several trees to take root on a nurse log, and the future result is a straight line of trees called a colonnade. These "trees on stilts" are characteristic of a temperate rain forest.

Although the western slopes of the Olympics can be deluged with up to 200 inches of annual precipitation, the eastern side of the Olympic Peninsula is protected by the rain shadow effect of the mountains. The town of Sequim (pronounced "Squim"), just forty miles from Mt. Olympus, receives only 15 inches of annual precipitation.

11

From the Rain Forests to the Summits

Walking up the river valleys of the Olympic Peninsula allows you to witness a variety of habitats in a relatively short distance. The rain forest quickly gives way to the lowland forest. Here the Sitka spruce is replaced by Grand Fir and Western hemlock becomes the most dominant tree. Western redcedar is also plentiful but disappears as you pass through the 3,000 foot level.

The montane zone begins where the redcedar ends. This zone is wetter, colder, and gets much more precipitation in the form of snow during winter. Silver fir is the dominant tree on the western slopes, while, due to the rain shadow effect of the mountains, Douglas fir becomes more prevalent on the eastern slopes.

The subalpine zone begins between 3,500 feet and 4,500 feet depending on location–higher in the drier, northeastern part of the peninsula. Subalpine fir, mountain hemlock, Douglas fir, and Alaska-cedar can all be found in various subalpine settings. Winter snows pile deep in the subalpine zone, and tree growth is slow.

The alpine regions of the Olympic Mountains receive a phenomenal amount of snow. No trees grow here. Glaciers, rock, melt ponds and meadows of wildflowers are what you find if you venture this high.

It is possible, in a day's time, to hike from the rain forest to the alpine zone, and on to any number of summits in the Olympic Mountains. Every 500 feet gained in elevation is equivalent to traveling 100 miles north. To put this in perspective, walking from the rain forest near sea level to the summit of Olympus at 7,965 feet would be the equivalent of traveling from Washington state to the Arctic on level ground.

A Wealth of Activities

The Olympic Peninsula has much to offer the outdoor enthusiast. From the 600 miles of trails in Olympic National Park, to the lakes, rivers, and myriad peaks on the Olympic Peninsula, the diversity of outdoor activities is great. Hiking, rafting, fishing, climbing, cross-country skiing, and mountain biking are all popular here. But it is the river systems–those arteries of the land, bringing life along their course, from the heart of the peninsula to the sea, that steal the show. At least for me.

Part I

Pacific Ocean Streams

Small boats are a fun way to explore Olympic peninsula streams.

Wynoochee River

The wettest weather station in the contiguous United States is located on the Wynoochee River, with an average annual precipitation of 144.43 inches. Located on the southern end of the Olympics, the Wynoochee River gently flows from Lake Wynoochee to its confluence with the Chehalis River near the town of Montesano. Above the lake, the Wynoochee continues on for a few miles and it is possible to put in a canoe below Wynoochee Falls to float down to Koho campground at the far end of the reservoir. Depending on the direction of the wind, this may mean a *lot* of paddling. As always, beware of big open water in a canoe, especially if the craft is heavily loaded. Above the falls, the Wynoochee quickly shrinks into a small stream.

Access to the Wynoochee River is via the Wynoochee Road, which follows the river for much of its fishable length. However, the river runs through farmland, and bank access is limited. Most of the fishing on the Wynoochee is done from boats.

The Wynoochee is an excellent summer steelhead stream.

Fishing the Wynoochee

The fall months see the return of chinook, coho, and chum salmon, and sometimes the fishing is very good on the Wynoochee for these salmon species. But the Wynoochee River's claim-to-fame are the steelhead that return throughout its 10 month open season (closed April and May).

Both summer and winter steelhead return in good numbers on this river. There are so many winter streams on the Olympic Peninsula, the Wynoochee often gets lost in obscurity, but during summer this little river shines and is often one of the best producing steelhead streams on the Peninsula.

Summer flows on the Wynoochee are mellow, allowing for light tackle. Medium-weight spinning gear is adequate for spinner and spoon fishing. Fly anglers should take floating lines or the lightest of sinking tips. The standard down-and-across approach with your favorite summer steelhead flies will do the trick if you find some willing fish.

Floating the Wynoochee

There are no real hazards to boaters with basic skills. The occasional sweeper tree is the only real problem this river throws at you during normal flows. When the fishing is slow, a lazy summer float down the Wynoochee is still worthwhile.

Boat launches are located at Black Creek, three miles upstream from the U.S. 12 bridge, and another is found six miles beyond that. In addition, drifters with smaller boats can launch at a few points where the river comes in contact with the Wynoochee Road further upstream.

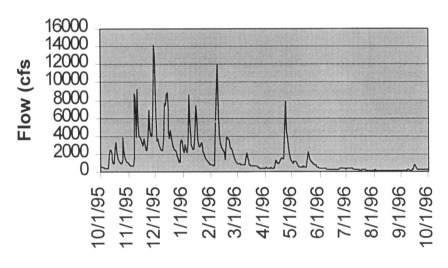

Wynoochee River Flow

Station 12037400 near Montesano

Other Activities

Boating and summer recreation is popular at Lake Wynoochee, but the fishing found there is nothing to write home about. There is a campground located at Lake Wynoochee.

Wynoochee (Lower)

Continued on page 20

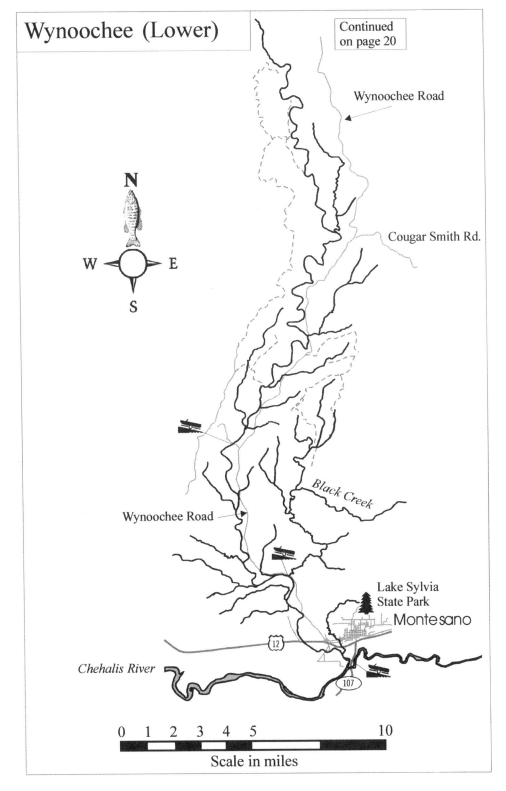

Wynoochee Road

Cougar Smith Rd.

N

W E

S

Black Creek

Wynoochee Road

Lake Sylvia State Park

Montesano

12

Chehalis River

107

0   1   2   3   4   5   10

Scale in miles

Wynoochee (Upper)

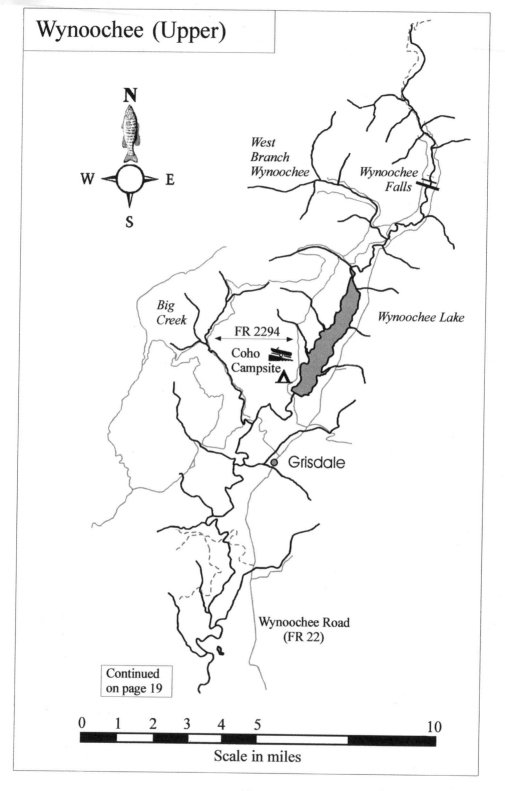

West
Branch
Wynoochee

Wynoochee
Falls

Big
Creek

FR 2294

Coho
Campsite

Wynoochee Lake

Grisdale

Wynoochee Road
(FR 22)

Continued
on page 19

| 0 | 1 | 2 | 3 | 4 | 5 | | | | 10 |

Scale in miles

Satsop River

Draining the southern Olympics, the Satsop River is comprised of the west and east forks which join a few miles north of the town of Satsop, just off U.S 12. The lower river meanders for several miles through farmland as it gently flows to its confluence with the Chehalis River, a few miles beyond the U.S. 12 crossing.

The most noted for fishing is the East Fork Satsop. East Satsop Road follows the river, leaving U.S. 12 four miles west of Elma and continuing to Schafer State Park, about eight miles distant. There are a limited number of bank access points along the way.

Fishing the Satsop River

Salmon Fishing

At one time, the Satsop was a good steelhead producer. Those days are long gone. Salmon fishing is the draw these days, and the returns are often large. So are the crowds. Most bank fishing is done in only a few holes. The river runs, for the most part, through private property.

Finding a spot along the river to fish is simply a matter of finding a wide spot in the East Satsop Road (there will usually be a concentration of cars) and following the trail down to the river. Prime stances along the good holes are valued, so be advised to stake your claim early or you may find yourself without a spot at all.

A Satsop River coho salmon.

During the peak of the run it is possible to catch chinook, coho, and chum salmon all in the same day. Most anglers use bait, but spinners, spoons and flies also work well when the fish are in thick and there is sufficient water for the fish to move steadily upstream. When this is the case, there is no need to leave your valued little piece of real estate – stick with it and let the fish come to you.

Finding the rivers in shape to fish is usually the biggest challenge of salmon fishing. Summers and early fall in western Washington are usually dry. When the fall rains do come, they typically arrive as a deluge, blowing the rivers out of shape. The salmon scream upstream to the hatcheries or spawning grounds, home free, so to speak.

The ideal situation would be for enough rain to raise the rivers so the fish can move, yet not dirty or push the water beyond fishable conditions. Sometimes this does happen, and it is the lucky angler on the stream when it does. To increase your chances, learn about the rivers you fish so that you know what flows translate to good fishing. Many streams have gauging stations that produce real-time data that you can access with a phone call or an internet connection.

Trout Fishing

The upper stretches of the East Fork Satsop, the West Fork Satsop, and many of the smaller tributary streams hold some special surprises for anglers willing to put in the hours exploring those reaches. I have friends who fish this area and have taken cutthroat over 20 inches in length and that's a big cutthroat anywhere! Of course, the average is much smaller.

Native cutthroat in these small coastal streams are willing feeders and will rise to nearly any properly fished dry fly. Walking one of these streams on a summer evening, and casting a small Elk Hair Caddis into pockets and riffles will help you understand why so many people are learning to fly-fish. Get out a topographical map, grab a light rod and a handful of flies, and explore the headwaters. The rewards may astound you.

Floating the Satsop

One way to escape the hoards of salmon anglers upstream is to drift the Satsop and fish the sections without bank access by boat. Boat ramps are located at Schafer State Park, right at the U.S. 12 Bridge, and near the confluence with the Chehalis River. This is straightforward floating, the only hazards being sweepers or a thicket of anglers standing in the river, either of which could snag the careless drifter.

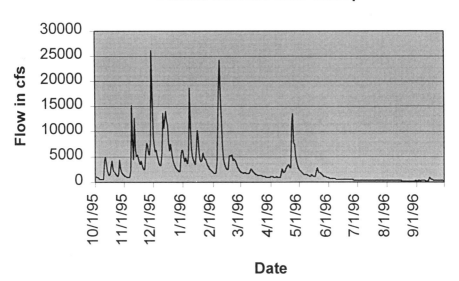

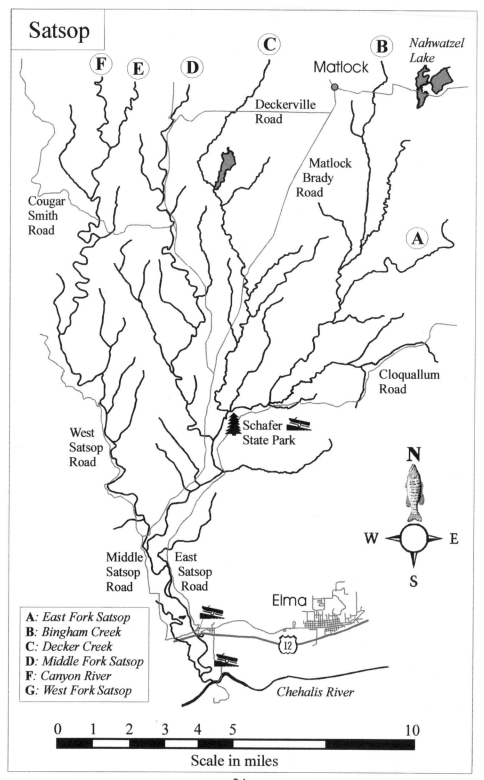

Satsop

Nahwatzel
Lake

C

B

F E D

Matlock

Deckerville
Road

Matlock
Brady
Road

Cougar
Smith
Road

A

Cloquallum
Road

West
Satsop
Road

Schafer
State Park

N

W E

S

Middle
Satsop
Road

East
Satsop
Road

Elma

A: *East Fork Satsop*
B: *Bingham Creek*
C: *Decker Creek*
D: *Middle Fork Satsop*
F: *Canyon River*
G: *West Fork Satsop*

12

Chehalis River

0   1   2   3   4   5   10

Scale in miles

Humptulips River

Draining the southern Olympics, the Humptulips River takes a south-westerly flow, traveling some 50 miles before emptying into Grays Harbor. There are two main tributaries, the West and East Forks, which are joined by several feeder streams along the way. The most significant of these is Stevens Creek, which enters the Humptulips in the last third of the river's course. Above the confluence of the two main forks, the Humptulips branches are obviously much smaller streams.

Access to the upper river, the West and East Forks, is via Donkey Creek Road (West Fork) and East Humptulips Road (East Fork). Logging roads which spur from these may also be open for additional access, but permission may be required. The best way to figure an approach is to scrutinize a copy of *Washington Atlas & Gazetteer*, by the DeLorme Mapping Company, or the appropriate topographic maps.

The lower river is accessed via the Copalis Crossing Road off Highway 101 at the town of Humptulips.

When it comes to fishing, the "Hump," as it is locally known, is most noted for the returns of the anadromous species: steelhead, salmon, and sea-run cutthroat trout.

Below the Highway 101 Bridge, the Humptulips meanders towards the ocean, bordered by the ever-present tangle of western Washington vegetation. This lower section of the Humptulips is best fished by boat. Nearly any floating craft will suffice, as the river below the confluence of the two forks is slow-paced. The only real challenges for the floater are a chute at the Humptulips hatchery and the jet-sleds which scream up and down the river. Drift boats and inflatable personal boats are ideal for fishing the "Hump."

There are a small number of summer steelhead taken on the Hump but this river doesn't really get active until fall. Most noted over the years are the returns of large chinook salmon which show up in September and continue throughout the fall. Many Washington anglers consider the Hump to be the best salmon river in the state. It is not unusual to catch these monsters all the way into November.

Traditionally, coho and chum salmon fishing has also been very good here. These fish begin to show in good numbers by October, and stragglers can still be found into January. During the peak of the run all three species are available at the same time. Check current regulations before fishing since these fish are being managed carefully to avoid depletion.

Fishing the Humptulips

Salmon

Trolling for salmon is very popular in the lower Humptulips. The river is only open to the taking of these fish from the mouth to the confluence of the East and West Forks. It's so popular when the fall salmon are present, the river is often crowded. Virtually all types of salmon gear is used by the hordes of anglers here. One definitely needs to be in the frame of mind for "combat angling."

Bait, spinners, spoons, plugs – everyone has their favorite methods for catching these fish.

Steelhead

When it comes to the steelhead fishing, the winter months produce well along the entire system. Again, floating is popular on the lower river. Bank anglers do well fishing the stretch around the hatchery, which is about two miles below the Highway 101 Bridge.

Above the forks, the Humptulips is more suited to lighter tackle and a variety of techniques. Fine fly-fishing water can be found here, as the streams are much smaller, with well defined and approachable holding water. The low, clear water often warrants a cautious approach and sized-down flies or other terminal tackle. As with most of the Olympic Peninsula rivers, the large native steelhead make their appearance in the later winter months.

At one time summer steelheading was productive here, and although smolts are still planted, the returns fall way short of their winter counterparts.

Sea-run Cutthroat / Resident Trout

Sea-run cutthroat enter the river in July and remain throughout the late fall and winter. The entire river system can be good for these anadromous trout. Fly and spinner angling is especially productive.

Search the stagnant pools, around root wads and other structure for sea-runs. Attractor wet flies and almost any small spinner will entice these fish once you find them.

Resident cutthroat can be found during the open season, especially above the forks and in the smaller tributaries. These smallish trout are willing risers to just about any dry fly.

Floating the Humptulips

There is a boat ramp right at the Highway 101 Bridge, and a couple upstream, off the East Humptulips and McNutt Roads. On the lower river, there are a few places to launch off the Copalis Crossing road, and a paved launch a mile or so above the mouth.

Floating the lower river is straight-forward, with no rapids. One should always use caution during high water periods and after storms, keeping sweepers and other storm related hazards in mind.

Floating the Humptulips.

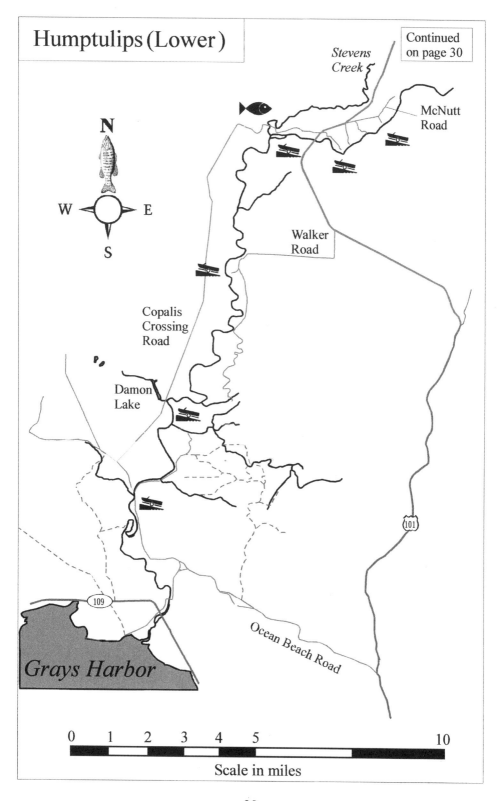

Humptulips (Lower)

Continued on page 30

Stevens Creek

McNutt Road

N

W E

S

Walker Road

Copalis Crossing Road

Damon Lake

101

109

Grays Harbor

Ocean Beach Road

| 0 | 1 | 2 | 3 | 4 | 5 | | | | | 10 |

Scale in miles

29

Humptulips (Upper)

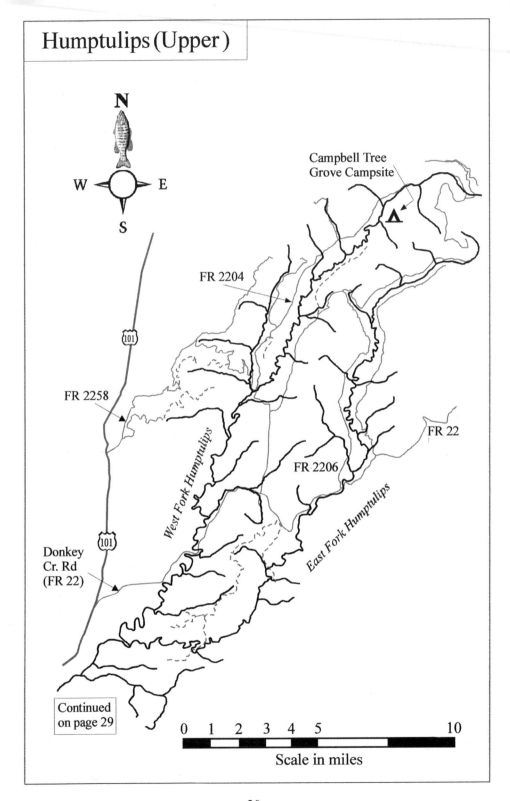

Campbell Tree
Grove Campsite

FR 2204

FR 22

FR 2258

FR 2206

West Fork Humptulips

East Fork Humptulips

Donkey
Cr. Rd
(FR 22)

Continued
on page 29

0 1 2 3 4 5   10

Scale in miles

Quinault River

  The Quinault River is one of the larger rivers draining the Olympics, emptying into the Pacific Ocean. The main Quinault, the North Fork, and numerous smaller tributaries reach deep within the southern peaks, gathering strength along the way. Culmination of the upper river ends as it spills into big Lake Quinault. The river below the lake takes on water from a few more tributaries before emptying into the ocean at the town of Taholah.

  Access to the upper river is via the South Shore and North Shore Roads which skirt their respective sides of the lake and river. Both roads are only paved about half of the way upriver. The South Shore Road is by far the better road, and is the one to take if you are pulling a trailer. About 10 miles past the east end of the lake, the roads meet at a modern bridge crossing the river.

  If you continue past the bridge on the South Shore Road approximately 5 miles, you come to the end of the road at Graves Creek Campground. If you pass the bridge traveling upstream on the North Shore Road, it is about 3 miles to the end of the road at the North Fork Campground.

Ferns and moss dominate the rainforest understory.

An Olympic cascade.

Beaver Falls.

Olympic Peninsula rainbow trout.

Pinky Freeman releasing a Satsop chum.

Winter Steelhead

The steelhead attraction in the Upper Quinault is for the large, native fish that arrive during the latter part of the winter season. The river is open from the park boundary down to the lake, and, during the months of February and March, several die-hard "big fish" hunters try their hand.

This is not easy fishing. The small number of returning fish combined with the crystal-clear water make for demanding steelheading. You must do everything perfectly, including holding your mouth just right.

Since the fish are native, and large, you might think that stout tackle would be in order as is typical when fishing for late-season, native fish. Not so. In fact, lighter lines and smaller baits are usually called for because of the clear water. Combined with the swift flow of the Upper Quinault, you will have your hands full if you are lucky enough to get a big native to strike.

There are not as many prime holes or classic holding waters on the Upper Quinault as you might find on some rivers, but those "fishy" spots that you do come across deserve special and thorough attention. This is the kind of water where you should try several different lures, flies, or whatever it is you are using. Don't leave a hole until you are satisfied you've given it your best.

There are only a few points where the upper river comes in contact with, or even comes close to, the North or South Shore Roads. For this reason, most of the steelhead fishing on the river is done by boat. Aggressive shore-bound anglers can still find water to fish, but they must be willing to work at it. This translates into a lot of walking.

Trout

Most Olympic Peninsula rivers are not famous, or even well known, for their trout fishing. It would be a stretch to say the Quinault is either, but both the North Fork and the mainstem Quinault host decent populations of rainbow trout, Dolly Varden, and whitefish. In addition, the mainstem contains eastern brook trout.

Trails follow both forks of the Quinault past the campgrounds. The main stem trail follows the stream for at least 15 miles into Enchanted Valley. This is a perfect place to cast dry flies to the plentiful, but small, trout. A 12-incher is a prize! Occasionally, a larger Dolly Varden is landed, but remember, they are protected, and must be released unharmed.

Whitefish

The same tactics you use for trout will work for these scrappy fighters. Often, the angler doesn't know their hooked fish isn't a trout until they see it. Try dry flies and small nymphs for the best action.

Lake Quinault

Lake Quinault is located on the reservation, so a tribal permit is required if you want to fish there. It's a beautiful lake, and some nice cutthroat, rainbows, and Dolly Varden come from its depths, but not in numbers. Most of those who have decent fishing have paid their dues – they have put in the hours.

Floating the Upper Quinault

It is important to keep in mind that the Upper Quinault is no different than any other large Olympic Peninsula river in that it is subject to immense stream-bed flooding during times of major winter storms. There are usually several such storms each winter season. With that said, the upper river poses no real obstacles to the floater at the time of this writing, providing they use common sense and have moderate river navigation abilities.

It is always a good idea to check with other floaters about hazards, and keep your eyes open for potential problems. Pay particular attention to sweepers and log jams. These get more Olympic Peninsula floaters in trouble than anything else.

Most drifters launch at the bridge on the Upper River, and take out at the point where the river comes close to the North Shore Road. Some floaters, however, take out at the point where the river comes close to the South Shore Road. Still others float all the way to the lake, and row to the boat launch located on the southeast shore. The amount of time available and personal ambition will determine the length of your float.

Hiking And Other Activities

The Lake Quinault region has long been an area of the Olympics big on recreation. Opportunities range from the famous Lake Quinault Lodge and recreation on the lake itself to the trails and peaks in the area that are a main attraction to hikers and climbers.

The Colonel Bob Trail spurs from the South Shore Road, but of more popular concern to the recreating public are the trails that follow the Quinault River, both the North Fork and the main stem.

The North Fork Trail follows the river for several miles, providing access to fishermen as well as backpackers and climbers seeking access to some of the southern Olympic peaks.

One of the most popular hikes in the Olympic National Park is up the Enchanted Valley. A prettier hike would be tough to find. From the Graves Creek Campground this moderate trail follows the main stem Quinault through the rain forest, past giant Sitka Spruce and western hemlock (including the record hemlock 15 miles in), and eventually steepens to reach Anderson Pass (4,464 ft.) about 18 miles from the trailhead. From here, climbers can access several popular routes.

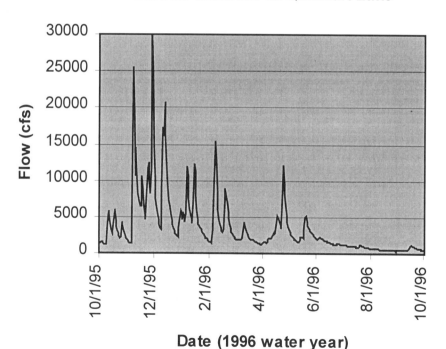

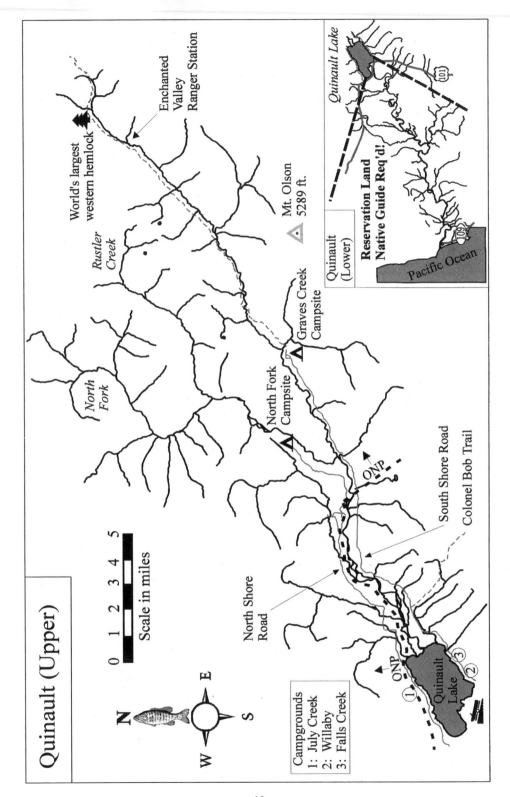

Quinault (Upper)

Scale in miles
0 1 2 3 4 5

N E S W

Campgrounds
1: July Creek
2: Willaby
3: Falls Creek

World's largest western hemlock

Enchanted Valley Ranger Station

Rustler Creek

North Fork

Mt. Olson 5289 ft.

North Fork Campsite

Graves Creek Campsite

ONP

North Shore Road

South Shore Road

Colonel Bob Trail

ONP

Quinault Lake

Quinault (Lower)

Quinault Lake

Reservation Land Native Guide Req'd!

Pacific Ocean

101

109

Clearwater River

The Clearwater River is a free-flowing tributary of the Queets which flows from the north and joins the lower Queets River at the Queets/Clearwater Bridge. This is the last exit point on the Queets before the river flows into the Quinault Indian Reservation where native guides are required. Access to this slow moving river is good. The Clearwater Road parallels the river for a dozen miles and numerous smaller roads approach the river.

Fishing the Clearwater

Salmon / Steelhead

There are some chinook salmon entering the Clearwater in the fall, but the slow water is more suited for the coho which return in October and November. Patient anglers catch a few of these, but current regulations require that they be released.

The return of wild winter steelhead, although not in great numbers, is the real attraction here. This river is not planted with hatchery smolts, so be prepared to release these wild steelhead unharmed. The usual patterns and tactics apply on the Clearwater. The slightly slower water allows for less encumbering weight and more enjoyable casting.

Trout

There is little in the way of resident trout in the Clearwater, but sea-run cutthroat can be found during the fall for those willing to search them out.

Floating the Clearwater

There is a rough boat launch located on the upper Clearwater approximately 13 miles upstream. Fives sets of mild rapids must be negotiated if you intend to float the distance to the take out at the confluence with the Queets River. Although listed as rapids on some maps, these areas are no more than short stretches of heavy riffle water which can be easily navigated with moderate boating skills.

Clearwater

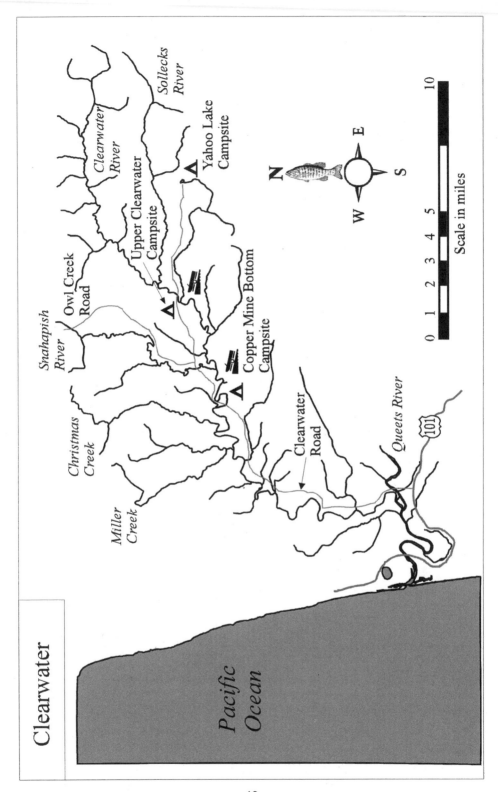

Pacific Ocean

Clearwater River

Sollecks River

Yahoo Lake Campsite

Upper Clearwater Campsite

Owl Creek Road

Snahapish River

Christmas Creek

Miller Creek

Copper Mine Bottom Campsite

Clearwater Road

Queets River

101

N
W E
S

0 1 2 3 4 5 10
Scale in miles

42

Queets River

The River

Many of the native tribes that lived on the Olympic Peninsula believed that within the center of the Olympic Mountains lived the legendary Thunderbird, possibly the most important figure in Pacific Northwest native mythology. Where the Thunderbird lived, the natives refused to travel. So, even though the native people had lived on the Olympic Peninsula for thousands of years, it wasn't until white explorers started poking around in the late 1800s that the interior of the Peninsula was explored. Until that time, the headwaters of the famous and not so famous rivers were sacred. Hopefully, we will regain some of that reverence before it is too late. Of all the special streams on the Peninsula, possibly the most renowned is the Queets.

The Queets river is born deep within the Olympic Mountains. It starts as meltwater from the Queets Glacier on Mt. Queets and the Humes and Jeffers glaciers on Mt. Olympus, plus the drainage from the snowfields of Dodwell-Rixon Pass (named for a survey party that explored much of this rugged territory). Also fed by significant tributaries, including Tsheletsky, Sams, Matheny and Salmon Creeks, and the Clearwater River, the Queets travels some 50 miles before emptying into the Pacific Ocean.

And what a wild journey it can be. With roots deep within the Olympics, and traveling through a temperate rain forest with annual precipitation of 12 feet, the runoff can punch the river out of shape during times of storm, taking several days to recover. As a result of the more severe winter storms (there are a few each season), the river channel is constantly changing. The awesome power of moving water is displayed by old growth timber piled along the shores and in jams, or a dry section of river bed, replaced by a totally new channel carved through ancient timber a quarter mile away.

The constant changing river channel made it hard for the early settlers who homesteaded along the Queets. Although the land was fertile, it was not uncommon for years of land clearing and grooming to be swallowed up by the river in a single winter season. It was a tough existence, to say the least.

But even this meager existence for the homesteaders along the Queets was short lived. In his early exploration of the Olympic Peninsula in 1885, Lt. Joseph P. O'Neil concluded that this territory was "absolutely worthless except for scenery and game." He suggested the Olympic Peninsula be set aside as a National Park. In 1938, President Franklin D. Roosevelt declared much of it just that. As a result, those pioneer families whose homesteads were within the boundaries of the new National Park were forced to give up their land. Many completely left the area.

The wet, mild climate found in the Queets River Valley is, of course, responsible for the profusion of plant life and the majestic trees of the rain forest. It is in the Queets Valley where a behemoth Douglas Fir, once the largest known of its species, stands. Storms broke the top off of this giant, but, at its base, this magnificent tree measures seventeen feet in diameter and is estimated to be 202 feet tall to its broken top.

Fishing the Queets

The Queets is one of the best known steelhead waters on the Olympic Peninsula. The biggest draw of anglers results from the huge annual plant of steelhead smolts in the Salmon River, a lower tributary. In addition to the hatchery steelhead, the Queets hosts some of the largest native steelhead in the state, as well as summer steelhead, chinook and coho salmon, Dolly Varden, and sea-run cutthroat trout.

Winter Steelhead

Since the waters of the Queets are of glacial origin, most of the time the river is milky. Visibility on a typical winter day might only be two feet. For this reason, most anglers use large, flashy lures or flies. The exception is during times of very cold weather when glacial melt is at a minimum, but this doesn't happen too often.

The winter run of steelhead usually get underway in November, with the big "Salmon River" return beginning in December and peaking in January. During this time, most of the action is on the lower river below the Salmon's confluence with the Queets. Phenomenal catches of hatchery steelhead draw anglers from the woodwork.

The section of the lower Salmon River which flows through the Olympic National Park is open to public fishing as is the section from the mouth to the Quinault Indian Reservation boundary. You need a tribal permit to fish above the boundary to the Q1000Rd Bridge, and a native guide above that point. These few miles of small stream steelheading give the wading angler outstanding fishing for hatchery fish. It may sound like a "fish story" but, if you hit things just right, 20 fish days are possible. That's good steelheading by any standard. For information or permits to fish the Salmon River, contact the Quinault Indian Reservation at (360) 276-8211.

Early in the season, it is the lower stretches of the Queets that are often fished the most, primarily due to the Salmon River return. The best access is by floating but the wading angler can gain access by walking down the Salmon to the mouth and working downstream along the bank.

There is a gravel road that parallels the river from Highway 101 to the Queets Campground, 13 miles distant. Along the way there are several places where the wading angler can make way to the river. A bit of determination is required to reach many of the good runs, but some are relatively easy. The easiest points of access, as you might guess, are at the boat launches along the river and those areas where the river comes close to the road. My favorites are the areas around the two rapids found on the Queets; Lyman and Sam's (see map).

By December there are usually fish throughout the river system, so it is not just the lower stretch that deserves attention. Even though bigger numbers of fish will come from the stretch below the Salmon River, native fish can be found in lesser numbers throughout the system.

Many of the rivers of the Olympic Peninsula, the Queets included, still host healthy runs of native steelhead. The obvious reason for this is that the headwaters, the spawning grounds, are located within the boundaries of a

National Park, protected from the ravages of logging, agriculture, and development. Most of the large, native fish return later in the season, from February through March or April. Once, while floating the Queets, I witnessed an angler land a large steelhead which he promptly smacked on the head. The large fish pegged his pocket scale that registered to 28 lbs. Although the current fishing regulations may state otherwise, all native fish (those without a clipped adipose fin) should be released unharmed. It is simply the right thing to do if we want to continue to have these magnificent fish in our rivers.

A chrome-bright steelhead from the Queets.

I personally prefer fly-casting, even on large rivers like the Queets. But this certainly isn't the most effective way to fish this big river. It's probably more appropriate to use a standard casting or spinning outfit. Due to the size of the Queets, it is simply easier to cover the water with conventional tackle. Many of the guided trips spend a good deal of time "plugging" the numerous stretches that are suitable for this type of fishing. This technique basically involves pulling a Quikfish®, Flatfish®, or HotShot® plug behind the boat while rowing upstream slower than the current to give the plug action. In this way, the boat and plug work downstream at a slow speed. Also popular are spinner or spoon fishing, and bait fishing with fresh roe or sand shrimp.

There is plenty of water available for all types of fishing preferences and styles.

Even though not as practical on such big rivers, there are some stretches where the fly angler can have a shot at a winter steelhead by following a few common sense rules. Those rules are really quite simple: 1) use a big, flashy fly, and 2) keep it near the bottom. At least, those are *my* simple rules!

When fly-fishing the Queets, or any large river for that matter, I spend most of my energy working areas below riffles, along banks and current seams–in other words, areas where I know steelhead like to hold.

Most of the time I use somewhat unconventional fly-fishing tactics. Instead of the standard sinking, sinking-tip, or shooting-heads most fly-rod steelheaders use, I prefer a full-floating line with a long leader (12 feet).The typical setup uses the line to drag the fly to the bottom, while I use a short-line nymphing technique more commonly employed for trout fishing.

The technique is really quite simple, and in reality, isn't much different than basic drift fishing with spinning or casting gear. The basic idea starts with a heavily weighted fly attached to my long leader. It is cast into likely water and "dead drifted" along the bottom. To accomplish this, you must keep a short line. Once you are close to the target, the fly is cast, and with the rod held high, the fly and leader's drift is followed with the rod tip to avoid drag. The hook is set at any hesitation in the drift.

Summer Steelhead

Summer steelhead take a back seat to the more plentiful and popular winter runs of these anadromous rainbows on the Queets. However, this is not for lack of fish to target; the Queets hosts a healthy run of these silvery torpedoes. Summer fishing usually gets underway in June and continues through the fall. Although far fewer people engage in chasing the summer steelhead, it is a favorite time for many seasoned anglers. The advantages over winter angling are quickly become obvious if you give it a try:

- The summer flows are much milder and the river is easier to wade.
- Smaller tackle can be used and fly-fishing is much more effective.
- Sunny periods can be counted in days instead of hours.
- Summer is the perfect time to pack light and explore.
- No ice in your guides!

The list goes on. Many summer steelheaders downsize their rods and lines for the summer fish, not so much because the steelhead are smaller, because they are not. However, the gentler summer flow is much more forgiving and the fish are easier to control during the battle. Those extra large spoons and other baits are also downsized since the milder current will allow the smaller offering to get down into the strike zone near the bottom.

Most fly anglers stow their heavy shooting-heads in favor of full-floating lines, and the standard down-and-across approach with low-water style steelhead patterns takes its share of fish.

Due to glacial melt in the mountains, the flow of the Queets is a deep aqua color during summer. Contrasted with the green of the rain forest, and towering mountains in the distance, a prettier stream would be hard to find.

More anglers fish the upper stretches of the river during summer than during winter. The area around the Queets Campground, both above and below, is very popular. The campground itself is a good base. With the towering trees, lush vegetation, numerous riverfront campsites, and the scenic trails through the forest, it is also a great spot for those non-fishers to pass the time.

Salmon

When fall rolls around, salmon begin their natal journey upstream. Fishing for chinook commences in addition to the summer steelhead that can still be found. This is one of my favorite times on the river. The big-leaf maples, vine maples and alders put on a show of red and yellow, and although the rainy periods become longer and more frequent, there are plenty of warm sunny afternoons to enjoy the river.

Salmon can be taken with a variety of terminal tackle. Many anglers use the same gear they use for steelhead. Plugs, spoons, and bait are the most popular. Most anglers target the deeper pools below riffles, and the deep water along banks.

Although the salmon of the Olympic Peninsula have fared better than in many Pacific Northwest waters, they are still on an up-and-down course–their fate, shaky, to say the least. Just as with steelhead, I always encourage the release of all wild fish unharmed. It may also be the law, depending on where you fish, so before you plan your trip, it's best to contact the National Park Service at (360) 452-4501 for current regulations.

Sea-run Cutthroat and Dolly Varden

Sea-run cutthroat can be found from mid summer throughout the fall and winter. Anglers target these feisty scrappers with small spinners and spoons and attractor wet flies.

The trick to finding sea-runs is to fish the edges of pools, around structure, and if you can find it – "frog water." It's the stagnant, leaf-covered, still water that you don't usually associate with trout. Sea-run cutthroat are especially fond of these slack areas.

Perhaps the best time to target the sea-run cutthroat is after the salmon have entered the river. These salt-going cutthroat trout will follow the salmon with hopes of chowing down on deposited eggs. If you spot salmon in a pool, you can bet that sea-runs are close by.

Dolly Varden char are found in all parts of the river the entire year. They are usually caught by anglers fishing for steelhead or cutthroat. Sadly, these once plentiful fish of the west are quickly disappearing. Dollies are protected here, so if you catch one, admire it quickly and release it.

Floating the Queets

Even though the energetic angler can gain access to productive water with a little muscle power, fishing the Queets is best done by floating. Driftboats are by far the most common craft, but quality rafts or small personal boats with good oar systems are also adequate if the operator has the appropriate skills to operate them.

Always beware of logjams on the Queets and other Olympic streams.

Difficulties are relatively few for the floater. Only two rapids are encountered in the entire open section. The first is Sam's Rapid, a boulder garden located just below the launch at the Queets Campground. Under normal (fishable) water conditions, drift boaters or rafters with moderate skills can work through the boulders with no problems. If in doubt, boats can easily be walked through on the launch edge of the rapid. The second rapid is Lyman's, between the Streaters Crossing and Hartzell launches. Again, this is a straight-forward rapid under normal water conditions. And again, if your confidence and/or ability falls short, you can line a boat through on either side of the rapid. Both fall short of "white water" but there are plenty of protruding rocks that could give the beginning or careless drifter some trouble.

Much more difficult to maneuver (and more dangerous) are the log jams that can be found along the river, especially in the lower drift below the Salmon River. Each major storm seems to rearrange the log jams. The heavy flow of the Queets, even under fishable conditions, can suck a careless boater under one of these jams in the wink of an eye. Please beware, and give these areas a wide berth!

Along the Queets River Road, three major boat launches are found. Hartzell Creek is the first you come to after leaving Highway 101. Floaters who launch here float down to the Queets/Clearwater Bridge, taking out on the left side of the river, under the bridge. The lower 1/4 mile or so (about the last bend) before reaching the bridge flows through the Quinault Indian Reservation, and you must stop fishing. Also, make sure you exit on the left side, even though you will see driftboats on the right. Although just a rocky river bottom, this is private property and the owner has not always allowed access. The river beyond this point is on native land and off limits to the public. It is disheartening for the floater to exit here and witness a maze of gillnets just beyond the bridge–especially if it has been a slow day.

Midway between the Hartzell access and the campground launch at the end of the Queets River Road is Streaters Crossing launch. Each float, Hartzell to Bridge, Streater to Hartzell, or Campground to Streater is around five or six miles, and is the perfect distance for a leisurely float or a serious day of steelheading. Of course, the amount of time a drift will take largely depends on the river's flow and your stops for picnicking, fishing, etc. Obviously, the fast moving winter pace will take less time than the mellower flows of summer. Picnics are usually shorter, too!

Choosing which drift to float largely amounts to guessing how far up the river the fish will be. This is important, of course, assuming you are floating the river to fish in the first place. Many people float the river simply for the joy of floating. This is especially true during summer, when you can see canoes, kayaks, and rafters out enjoying the weather and all the rain forest has to offer, which certainly includes viewing the plentiful wildlife. This can include Roosevelt elk, deer, black bears, eagles and, if you're lucky, a cougar might pass within viewing range.

Tim Mondale negotiates the Queets.

Hiking and Other Activities

The Queets Campground is not the end of the road. Well, it is, so to speak, but it's certainly not the end of the trail – it's the beginning. Just past the campground a trail crosses the river and continues up the Queets for 16.1 miles. The tricky part is crossing the river. During summer levels this is usually not a problem. There is a fairly broad shallow section (well marked) not too far up the trail. If you're thinking about crossing during times of high water – forget it!

Rain forest trail along the Queets.

The trail leading up the river is a fairly easy hike, gaining little in elevation. It is a spectacular hike through the rain forest. Just 2.3 miles in, a short spur leads to that former record Douglas Fir – worth the hike alone! After a little over 5 miles, you come to Tshletshy Creek. This is a popular destination for the hiking fisherman. Tshletshy Creek marks the upper boundary for steelhead angling.

There are a limited number of campsites at Tshletshy Creek, and the general area is blessed with prime steelhead holding water. A trail leads up Tshletshy Creek, along Tshletshy Ridge, and eventually drops down to the North Fork Quinault River, just one of the beautiful hikes found in the Olympics.

Ambitious hikers can follow the Queets River Trail for several miles and, if the desire is there, eventually make it all the way to the flanks of Mt. Olympus. Most climbers, though, use the Hoh River approach.

Always popular in the rain forest are the photographic opportunities, and the Queets Valley is about as photogenic as it gets. One never needs to look far for another unique subject to photograph. Sam's Loop Trail (1/2 mile long) winds through the rain forest understory at the Queets Campground, and is a favorite spot among nature photographers.

Mountain biking is becoming increasingly popular everywhere, and the 13 mile long Queets River Road is no exception. A slow, leisurely pace while pedaling gives a whole different perspective to the awesome surroundings.

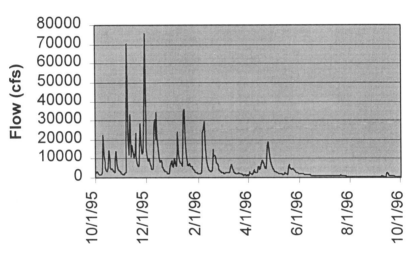

Queets River Flow
Station 12040500 near Clearwater

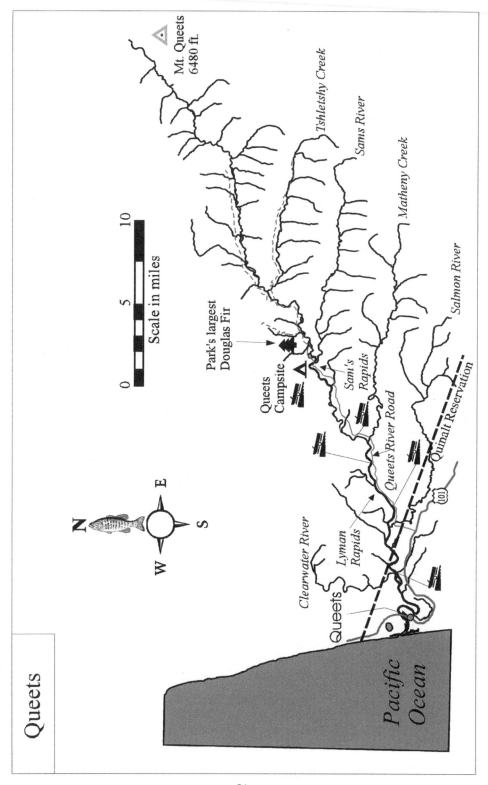

Queets

Mt. Queets
6480 ft.

Tshletshy Creek

Sams River

Matheny Creek

Salmon River

Park's largest
Douglas Fir

Queets Campsite

Sam's Rapids

Queets River Road

Quinalt Reservation

101

Clearwater River

Lyman Rapids

Queets

Scale in miles

0   5   10

N
W   E
S

Pacific
Ocean

Hoh River

When the early pioneer and settler, John Huelsdonk, "The Iron Man of the Hoh," amazingly found his way to the banks of the upper Hoh River and homesteaded back in the late 1800s, a new chapter in history began to unfold for this part of the Olympic Peninsula. Other settlers followed, but the ravages of the ever-changing Hoh River channel forced most away. Their toil of land clearing was often swallowed up by the river in one quick storm. The Huelsdonks, Andersons, and Fletchers are pioneer families who stayed, and descendants of these hardy pioneers are still living in the area.

John Huelsdonk homestead on the Hoh.

The three main branches of the Hoh begin deep within the Olympic Mountains. The North Fork (main fork) is fed by Mt. Tom Glacier, and gives the Hoh its distinct silty coloration. Humes Glacier feeds the South Fork, and Tom Creek joins between the two and is often called the Middle

Fork. The combination of these streams and the numerous creeks that drain this vast watershed make the Hoh the largest and wildest river of the Olympics.

Like the Queets and Quinault Rivers to the south, the Hoh winds its way through a temperate rain forest en route to the Pacific Ocean. Unlike the Queets and Quinault Rivers, only a small area near the mouth of the Hoh resides on native American reservation land, creating a tremendous stretch of public accessible water for recreation.

For reference, the Hoh is generally divided into two sections. That area above the Highway 101 Bridge is known as the Upper Hoh and, the area below, the Lower Hoh. Both sections are popular among floaters and fishermen alike.

About half of the Hoh's length falls within the boundaries of the Olympic National Park. From the rivers source down to around the park boundary, the Hoh runs wild and logjams occasionally span the entire river. Most angling and all floating is done from the park boundary downstream to near the mouth.

There are several campgrounds located along the Hoh River, especially on the Upper Hoh. Inside the National Park there is a large campground (Hoh) at the end of the road. Working downstream, you come to Morgan's Crossing, Willoughby and Oxbow. On the lower Hoh there is the Cottonwood Campground about three miles downstream from the Oxbow. In addition, many people camp on Nolan Bar, a popular take-out point two miles downstream from Cottonwood.

Fishing the Hoh

The Hoh is one of the most popular rivers on the Peninsula. Like most of the other western-flowing rivers of the Olympics, the Hoh's headwaters are deep within the National Park. Due to this protection, the spawning grounds and connected forests around them have remained untouched. This is one of the main reasons that runs of large, native, anadromous fish are still found here.

The fertile waters of the Hoh host both summer and winter steelhead, spring and fall chinook salmon, coho salmon, Dolly Varden, and sea-run cutthroat trout.

Access to the river for bank/wading fishermen is better than on most Olympic rivers. The Upper Hoh Road parallels the upper river for most of its length, from the Highway 101 crossing to the ranger station/visitor center, roughly 15 miles distant. The easiest access points are at the various boat ramps (see map) and at points where the river comes in close contact with the road.

The lower Hoh has fewer access points, as the road only travels close to the river in a few places. Cottonwood Camp and Nolan Bar (see map) are two popular areas for the boatless angler to gain access.

Winter Steelhead

You will find steelhead in the Hoh virtually every month of the year. However, it is the run of winter steelhead that gets the most attention on this river. The chance of catching trophy-sized steelhead of 20 pounds or better is probably why. Although native runs of large steelhead are diminishing everywhere, Olympic Peninsula streams like the Hoh still produce these brutes and are caught often enough for the word to get around. Of course, all native steelhead should be released unharmed to ensure the survival of this precious species. Well, I guess *all* species are precious, but I'll admit to having some favorites!

In addition to the native winter steelhead found in the Hoh, there is a very liberal plant of steelhead smolts, which accounts for most of the high number of fish bagged on this river.

The winter fish begin to show in November, and continue on through April, with the largest natives arriving during the latter part of the winter season.

Most boat anglers use the traditional "big river" methods on the Hoh. Pulling plugs along banks and broad flats is very popular. Drift fishermen do well, also, and certainly take their share of the fish.

Although the Hoh is a large, glacial river, there are several sections that lend themselves well to fly-fishing. There is an abundance of classic steelhead water (gradually tapering holding water) available to both the boat and wading angler.

Because of the silty coloration, large, flashy flies with plenty of movement are desirable. Bunny strip flies, large Buggers or any large winter pattern heavy on the flash and movement will work fine.

Early in the season, the entire river will hold fish. Later in the season, when the large natives return, many anglers prefer fishing the upper stretches (Upper Hoh) for a chance at one of these trophies.

Summer Steelhead

The Hoh is not planted with summer steelhead, but there are plenty of summer fish that return to this river. Hmm...I wonder if this means anything?

May will find summer steelhead venturing up the Hoh, with the peak of the run occurring in July. However, you can find good steelheading all summer and throughout the fall.

Although the Hoh River drains a large section of the Olympics and flows through a temperate rain forest, the heat of summer can drop the river's flow to a fraction of its winter levels. In addition, the warm summer sun causes increased glacial melt, adding to the silty water conditions.

The best summer steelheading opportunities are on cloudy days or during early morning and late evening hours. Even though the glacial coloration cuts the visibility to a couple feet, the steelhead here (like most places) will be more active during the low-light periods.

All types of conventional tackle work well here. Spinners, spoons, and plug fishing are especially popular. Medium weight rods are the standard.

During the summer months, the Hoh River gets more attention by fly-fishers than any other Olympic Peninsula river. The Hoh has long had a reputation as a good fly-rodding river. The numerous sections of pocket water, riffles, and classic holding water contribute greatly to this popularity.

Rods in the 7 to 8 weight range are the practical choice for summer fishing. Seldom is a head heavier than 200-grains needed, and many anglers even opt for a full-floater this time of year. Large, low-water steelhead flies are very popular.

Salmon

These days, salmon are not a predictable anadromous resource as they once were. There are a host of reasons this is so, not just on the Olympic Peninsula, but everywhere salmon are found. Anyway you look at it though, civilized, modernized, politicized man is a big part of the cause. Whew...got that off my chest!

Many of the smaller river systems with protected headwaters, like those found on the Olympic Peninsula, fare better than rivers where the headwaters are choked by dams, polluted by industry, or plagued by poor logging and agricultural practices.

Spring chinook are in the system for the opener in May, and trickle in throughout the early summer. They get quite a bit of attention, especially in the lower Hoh, where you can keep them. Most anglers pull plugs or toss big baits for these bruisers.

When the fall salmon start in, many are taken by steelhead anglers using typical steelhead tackle. Medium-weight steelhead rods using spinning or baitcasting reels loaded with 12 to 15 pound-test monofilament are the norm.

Although salmon can be taken on fly gear, especially coho, far fewer fly anglers are after them – most concentrate on the steelhead. Salmon catches are often incidental. If coho are your target, big flashy flies like the

Flash Fly, or brightly colored marabou patterns, are a good choice. A rapid pulsating retrieve can sometimes induce a powerful strike.

Sea-run Cutthroat and Dolly Varden

Fall through winter will find sea-run cutthroat concentrated in the deeper, slower water around structure such as logjams, pool edges, etc. Any small spinner or attractor wet fly will work for them.

Most of the Dolly Varden are caught incidentally, while fishing for sea-run cutthroat or steelhead. An ever-dwindling native fish, Dollies should always be released unharmed.

Floating the Hoh

Even though the Hoh has great access for the wading angler, floating is by far the preferred method for gaining access to this river.

Floating the Upper Hoh

The highest boat launch is located just inside the National Park boundary. Moving downstream you come to Morgan's Crossing. The Oxbow camp and launch is located at the point where Highway 101 crosses the river and, downstream from there is the Cottonwood launch. In addition, boats are launched along the upper river at several points where the river passes close to the Upper Hoh Road. On the lower river, Nolan Bar is a popular enter/exit point. The last exit downstream is a point on the lower river where the lower Hoh Road passes near the river.

Because of sweepers and logjams, the river inside the national park is unfloatable. The floatable section (from the highest launch to the mouth) is relatively straightforward with few obstacles. The most difficult sections are the area know as "The Gorge" on the upper river (see map), and the short rapids just above the Oxbow camp. Moderate river running skills are required for both of these areas under normal water flows. Drift boats and river rafts both work well if the operator has the skills for short stretches of water approaching Class lll under certain water flows.

During times of high water, the Hoh and all rivers of the Olympic Peninsula can be dangerous. Drifting trees, sweepers and logjams are definite hazards. The novice or absent-minded floater should not attempt this river.

Hoh River Flow
Station 12041200 at Hwy. 101

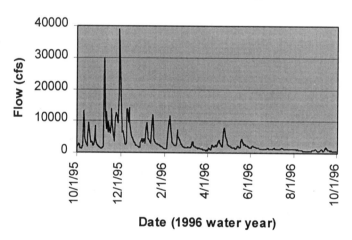

Date (1996 water year)

It is important to keep in mind that the Hoh River channel is in constant change. Several times each winter, powerful, drenching storms raise the Hoh to dangerous levels, overflowing its banks and changing the channel. As the water subsides, behemoth trees, log jams, and other obstacles are created. After times of high water, always approach this river with caution. When in doubt, contact the National Park Service, Washington Department of Fish and Wildlife, or other floaters about the current hazards.

Hiking and Other Activities

From the Hoh Rain forest Visitors Center it is 17.5 miles to Glacier Meadows – the end of the trail, on the flanks of Mt. Olympus. The easy access to this trail combined with the ease of hiking makes this one of the most popular trails in the park.

Sitka spruce, western redcedar, bigleaf maple, ferns and mosses of the rain forest create a canopy of intense green as you walk along the flat beginnings of the Hoh River Trail. Grassy meadows and alders are found at the camps located at points where the river comes in contact with the trail.

You come to a junction with the Hoh Lake trail in 9.8 miles. This 5.3 mile trail climbs steeply to the lake, and continues up the ridge joining the High Divide trail at 6.5 miles. The view from here is breathtaking. Moving up the Hoh Valley, western hemlock and Douglas-fir begin to outnumber the giant spruce trees. Huckleberries and salmonberries are found in good numbers along the trail during the appropriate season.

As the trail continues, a bridge spans the river at 13.5 miles as it rushes through a steep gorge. Shortly downstream it joins Glacier Creek, a significant tributary.

Once across the river the trail begins a steep ascent. At 15.2 miles, you arrive at Elk Lake and a camping area along the trail. Elk Lake provides good fishing for pan-sized brook trout.

From Elk Lake, the trail climbs through avalanche fields, then a forest of silver fir and Alaska-cedar, and eventually, at mile 17.5, the Glacier Meadows Campground. From this point a rough trail climbs past a ranger tent, through a subalpine forest and eventually to the terminal moraine of Blue Glacier. Soon the path leads to the lateral moraine and allows climbers access to the ice. Total distance from the trail head to the ice is close to 18 miles.

South Fork Hoh River

Reached via the Hoh-Clearwater Road off Highway 101, the South Fork Hoh trail begins at the end of DNR Road 1000. This four mile trail gives the angler great access to the South Fork. Trout, whitefish, Dolly Varden and steelhead are the attraction on this tributary which gets far less pressure than the main Hoh.

The South Fork usually runs clear except during times of heavy rain. It is often an ace-in-the-hole when the main river is blown. Treat this river kindly, and remember, the South Fork falls under catch-and-release regulations.

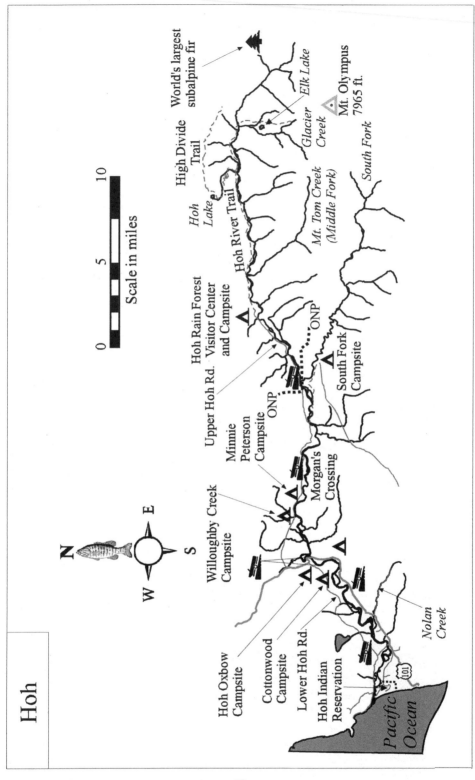

Hoh

Scale in miles
0 5 10

N
E
W
S

World's largest subalpine fir

High Divide Trail

Elk Lake

Glacier

Mt. Olympus 7965 ft.

Creek

South Fork

Hoh Lake

Hoh River Trail

Mt. Tom Creek (Middle Fork)

Hoh Rain Forest Visitor Center and Campsite

Upper Hoh Rd.

ONP

Minnie Peterson Campsite

ONP

South Fork Campsite

Morgan's Crossing

Willoughby Creek Campsite

Hoh Oxbow Campsite

Cottonwood Campsite

Lower Hoh Rd.

Hoh Indian Reservation

101

Nolan Creek

Pacific Ocean

Dickey River

The Dickey is a river tributary of the Quillayute System. The Dickey empties into the Quillayute River about a mile from the Pacific Ocean. To reach the fishable water, take the La Push road off Highway 101, just north of Forks, and turn right on the Mora Road to reach the mouth of the river. The upper portions of the river can be accessed from the Mina Smith Road, via the Quillayute Road.

Winter steelhead, chinook and coho salmon, and sea-run cutthroat trout can all be found in the Dickey River. Fall fishing can produce fair salmon and great sea-run cutthroat angling. The winter steelheading can be good at times, especially towards the end of the winter season. Although the Dickey is too small for boating, roadside foot access is intermittently available up the forks. The West Fork eventually leads to Dickey Lake.

Small stream winter steelhead.

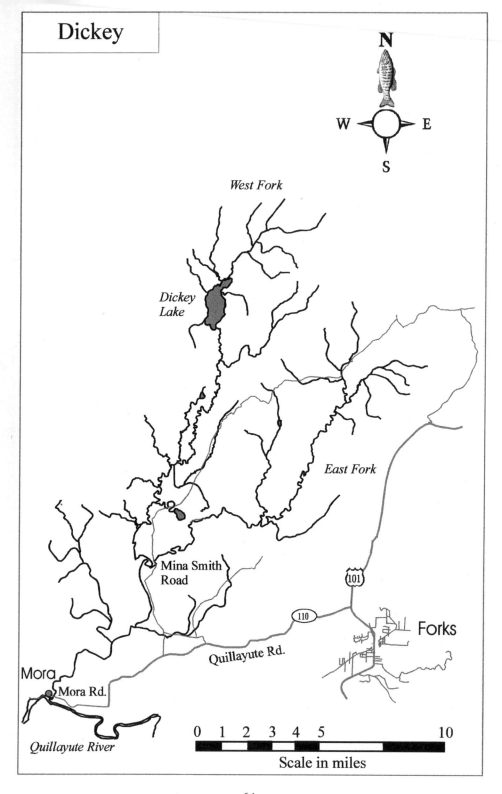

Dickey

West Fork

Dickey
Lake

East Fork

Mina Smith
Road

[101]

[110]

Forks

Quillayute Rd.

Mora

Mora Rd.

Quillayute River

| 0 | 1 | 2 | 3 | 4 | 5 | | | | | 10 |

Scale in miles

Sol Duc River

The Sol Duc is a fast-paced river that drains the northern Olympic Mountains. Eventually finding its way west, it joins forces with the Bogachiel River to form the Quillayute River which, after a short six miles, empties into the Pacific Ocean.

The Sol Duc travels an irregular course that is mostly followed by U.S. Highway 101, providing access along much of its course. However, most of this access is in the form of boat launches, as there is little bank access available.

From their sources high in the northern Olympics, the North Fork and Main Fork Sol Duc Rivers join forces and turn into one of the wildest rivers on the Peninsula. Seldom changing course by winter floods that effect many peninsula rivers, the Sol Duc's rocky bottom and deep channels help keep this river's channel fairly constant.

Bank access is poor along most of the Sol Duc. Private property and the dense coastal vegetation make it very difficult to fish this river except by boat. Most people who fish the Sol Duc do so with a guide. Even when floating the river, places to get out and wade are limited. Consequently, most fishing is done from a boat.

Fishing the Sol Duc

The Sol Duc is one of the fishiest rivers on the Olympic Peninsula. Winter and summer steelhead, spring and fall chinook, coho, chum, and sockeye salmon, plus Dolly Varden and sea-run cutthroat trout can all be found here.

Winter Steelhead

Winter steelhead are the main attraction on the Sol Duc. Annual catches are consistently strong, with anglers taking nearly 2,000 winter fish. The action usually gets underway in December, with the best fishing from January through April.

Hatchery fish provide the bulk of the action during the early winter season, but by late February though April, anglers have a good chance of catching large native fish. If it is a trophy-sized steelhead you are after, the Sol Duc is one of your best choices on the peninsula.

65

The Sol Duc is an excellent winter steelhead stream.

Every steelheading technique will work well on the Sol Duc. Many anglers use spinning or casting gear, but fly-fishing is also popular here. Since the Sol Duc is, for the most part, a fast paced river, heavier flies and/or lures should be considered.

Summer Steelhead

Summer steelhead are not planted in the Sol Duc and, although they take a backseat to the more numerous winter-run fish, the summer months yield enough fish to keep the die-hards coming back.

The Sol Duc during summer flow is quite a different river than during the winter. Although the river is still swift, more gravel bars are exposed and floating is extremely difficult in places because of exposed rocks. On the plus side, holding water is easy to spot and those who are adept at reading the water often do very well.

Obviously, lighter tackle can be used during the summer. Pocket water and riffles lead to various low-water tactics. The Sol Duc is especially accommodating to fly-fishers at this time. A good fly angler can do as well as any other technique during the low water season and the long rod is increasingly popular here.

Salmon Fishing

The Sol Duc is one of the best spring chinook rivers on the Olympic Peninsula. When the water conditions are right, the fishing can be great, but therein lies the problem. The water is often low and clear during the months of April, May and June; the height of the springer season. This makes for some tough fishing. The best scenario is to hit the river just after a good rain. Pulling plugs through the deeper holes and along banks is the most productive.

Fall salmon fishing can be good at times. Fall chinook and coho salmon are the prime targets for anglers. These fish begin to show in October when the fall rains begin, and continue on in numbers through November.

Sea-run Cutthroat and Dolly Varden

Sea-run cutthroat begin to enter the river late summer and continue throughout the fall and winter. Fish the edges of pools, around structure, and pay special attention to the "frog water"– that slow-moving, stagnant-looking water around the edges of pools or connecting sloughs.

Small spinners, spoons and attractor fly patterns work well for these aggressive cutthroat. Keep in mind that these are schooling fish. When you find one, there are probably more close by.

Dolly Varden can be found all year. Catches of these char are usually incidental, by steelhead, salmon or cutthroat fishermen. Dollies are protected on the Sol Duc, so if you catch one, release it carefully.

Floating the Sol Duc

I can not express enough caution to those wishing to float the Sol Duc. This is a fast paced river with plenty of hazards. There are six drifts on the Sol Duc, starting at Klahowya State Park and ending where the Sol Duc and Bogachiel meet. Each one of these drifts has Class II+ to Class III stretches, with rapids, narrow channels, and boulder gardens that require maneuvering. The Sol Duc is no place for the beginning boater. Even experienced boaters should use extreme caution, and I highly recommend going with a guide the first time.

Dolly Varden can be found all year. Catches of these char are usually incidental, by steelhead, salmon or cutthroat fishermen. Dollies are protected on the Sol Duc, so if you catch one, release it carefully.

Floating the Sol Duc

I can not express enough caution to those wishing to float the Sol Duc. This is a fast paced river with plenty of hazards. There are six drifts on the Sol Duc, starting at Klahowya State Park and ending where the Sol Duc and Bogachiel meet. Each one of these drifts has Class II+ to Class III stretches, with rapids, narrow channels, and boulder gardens that require maneuvering. The Sol Duc is no place for the beginning boater. Even experienced boaters should use extreme caution, and I highly recommend going with a guide the first time.

Immature male coho or chinook salmon such as this one that return with the spawning run are called "jacks."

Sockeye salmon.

Spawning salmon.

A male pink salmon or "humpy" in spawning form.

Coho salmon.

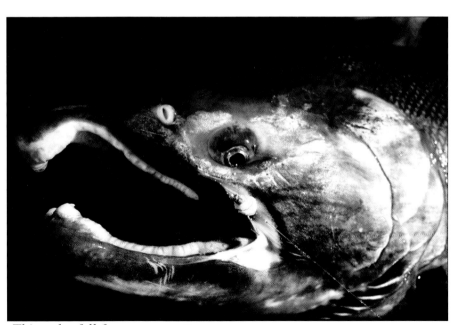

This coho fell for an egg pattern.

Ron Meek releasing an Olympic steelhead.

Dolly Varden char, named for a Charles Dickens character with a yellow polkadot dress.

The brook trout, also a char, is native to the eastern United States.

Rain forest trail on the Quinault.

Lake Quinault.

Queets River crossing.

The author examines the "Record" Douglas-Fir on the Hoh trail.

Hiking and Other Activities

High Divide Loop Tail

Perhaps one of the most beautiful and spectacular waterfalls in the Olympics is Sol Duc Falls (see back cover). Reached from Highway 101, the Sol Duc Hot Springs Road travels 13 miles past Sol Duc Hot Springs and Sol Duc Campground to its end and a parking lot. The trailhead begins here, and the broad trail travels for 0.7 miles through the bottomland forest to the falls.

The High Divide trail continues from here, making a 17.6 mile loop that is very popular with backpackers. The trail runs south from the falls and climbs to the alpine divide of the Hoh River, offering breathtaking views of Mt. Olympus and surrounding peaks. Several alpine lakes are passed along the way. The Hoh Lake trail spurs off the High Divide trail connecting to the Hoh River trail.

Sol Duc Falls.

Being so popular, a reservation system is in place for this hike. Permits are available at the Sol Duc Ranger Station.

There is also a trail leading up the North Fork Sol Duc for nine miles to its end. This is an unimproved trail, leading through a spectacular, undisturbed forest. Some walk the trail to fish, but the trout are mostly small.

Sol Duc (Lower)

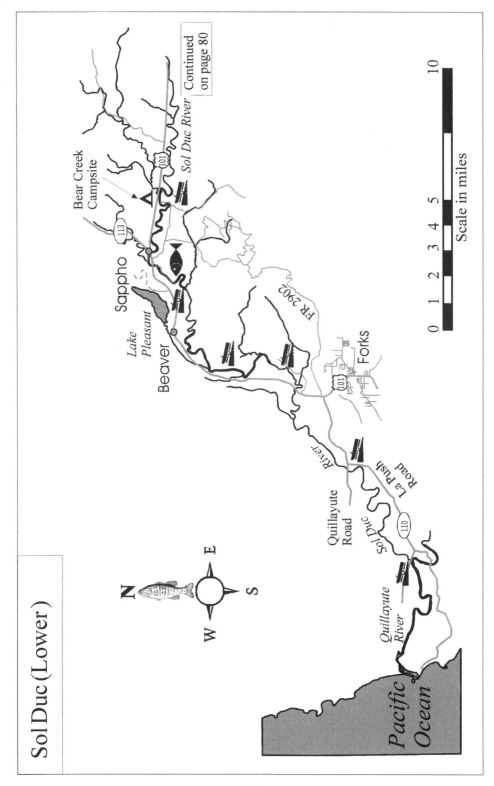

Continued on page 80

Scale in miles

79

Sol Duc (Upper)

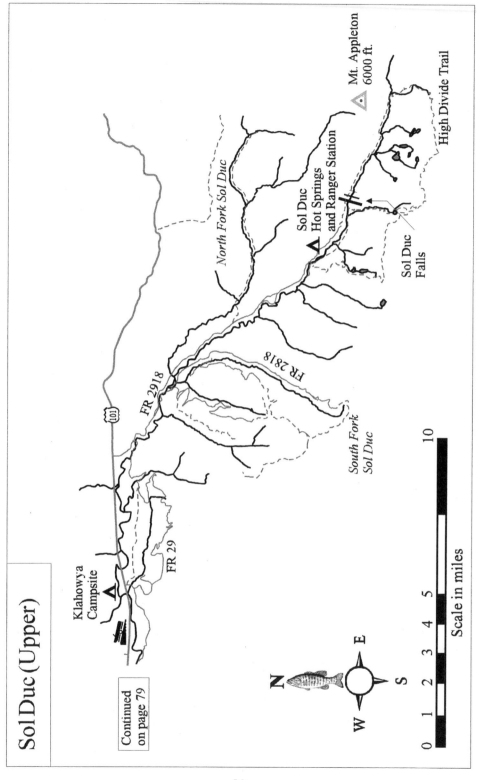

Continued on page 79

Klahowya Campsite

FR 29

FR 2918

North Fork Sol Duc

FR 2818

South Fork Sol Duc

Sol Duc Hot Springs and Ranger Station

Sol Duc Falls

Mt. Appleton 6000 ft.

High Divide Trail

N
E
S
W

Scale in miles

0 1 2 3 4 5   10

Calawah River

Forest Road 29, 1.5 miles north of the town of Forks, accesses the upper Calawah River. This Bogachiel River tributary is not a large stream, but it is an ace-in-the-hole for steelheaders in these parts, as it is one of the last rivers to muddy after a storm. In fact, it takes a heck of a storm to make this crystal clear stream unfishable.

Access to the upper reaches is good. Forest Road 29 follows the stream for seven miles to Hyas Creek, where the river splits into the North and South Forks. There are several places along this road where anglers can park and hike down to the river.

Fishing the Calawah

Steelhead

    Steelhead are the main attraction on this beautiful little river. Substantial quantities of both summer and winter fish are released by the State of Washington. Anglers need to consider the clarity of the water and use the appropriate gear. Lighter, longer leaders are necessary to avoid spooking the fish. Smaller lures or flies are called for, as is the case with most low, clear water situations.

    The Calawah falls under Selective Gear regulations; unscented flies or lures only with single, barbless hooks. Although the state still allow you to keep some wild steelhead, be responsible and caring, and release the ones you catch unharmed.

Winter steelheading on the Calawah.

    Deep pools, short tailouts and pocket water are the rule on the Calawah. A stealthy approach will certainly pay off for these steelhead, which are available every month of the year, except for May, when the river is closed.

Salmon

Fall coho are available in the Calawah if you hit it at just the right time. After the fall rains begin, salmon will move into the Quillayute River System, which includes the Calawah. Although not in great numbers, coho are often caught by steelheaders during the late fall and early winter.

Trout

Access to decent trout water on the Calawah is tough. It is only the upper stretches of the South Fork that produces, so I'm told. You can reach the upper river by hiking 6.1 miles on the Bogachiel trail, then 3.4 miles on the Indian Pass trail which climbs over Indian Ridge and drops down to the South Fork.

Floating the Calawah

There are a couple boat launches on the upper river, but this small stream can be very dangerous. Plenty of maneuvering is required to make it down in one piece. Guides float it during optimum water flows, and I would suggest floating with one first before attempting it on your own. A handful of kayakers enjoy the boulder gardens and fast chutes found on this river.

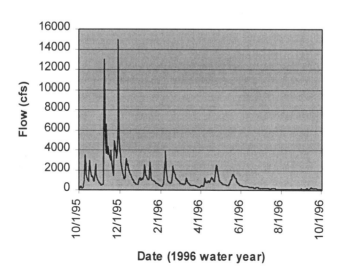

Calawah River Flow
Station 12043000 near Forks

Date (1996 water year)

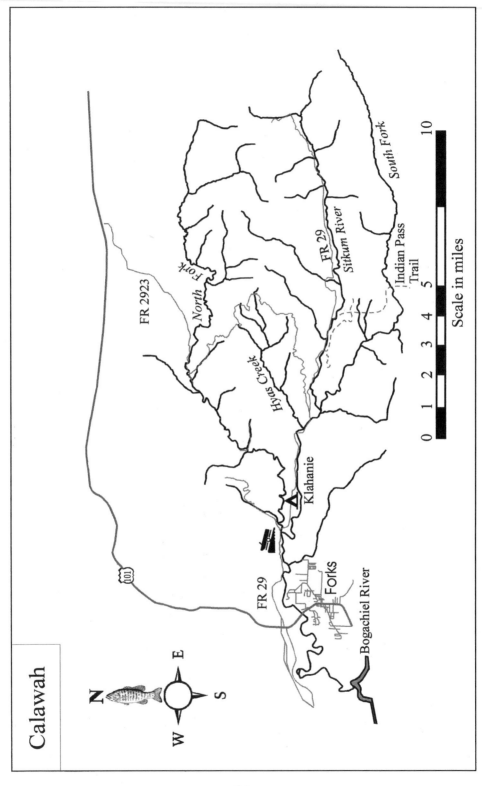

Calawah

N
W — E
S

Scale in miles
0 1 2 3 4 5 10

FR 2923

North Fork

Hyas Creek

Klahanie

FR 29

Forks

Bogachiel River

FR 29

Sitkum River

Indian Pass
Trail

South Fork

101

Bogachiel River

The word "Bogachiel" is from the native Quileute language. Roughly translated, it means "waters that become muddy following rainstorms." To winter steelheaders, this is often a frustrating fact.

One of the major rivers on the Olympic Peninsula, the Bogachiel drains a good portion of the northern Olympics. From the heart of the Olympic Mountains, the Bogachiel begins as the outflow of Bogachiel Lake. With it's beginning as the outflow of Rag Lake, the North Fork Bogachiel joins approximately ten miles distant, forming this river which is famous among northwest steelheaders.

Highway 101 crosses the Bogachiel River five miles south of the town of Forks. The upper river is reached via the North Bogachiel Road near this crossing, or by taking the South Bogachiel Road, a couple miles south of the crossing. Either road travels only a few miles. The South Bogachiel Road culminates at a boat ramp. The North Bogachiel Road ends at the Bogachiel River Trailhead, which follows the river for about 14 miles.

To reach the lower river take the La Push Road just north of Forks, or the Bogachiel Road at the south end of Forks, which leads to the Bogachiel Rearing Ponds.

Fishing the Bogachiel

The "Bogey," as it is locally known, is one of the most popular fishing destinations on the Olympic Peninsula. Although the river hosts chinook salmon and sea-run cutthroat trout, the majority of anglers descending on the Bogey are after the steelhead, both summer and winter-run fish.

Steelhead

December and January sees anglers flocking to the Bogachiel River following the tremendous runs of winter steelhead. Thousands of smolts are released each year from the Bogachiel Rearing Ponds. Their return causes a commotion on the Peninsula, for sure. When the water is fishable, the Bogey is one of the prime destinations for Olympic Peninsula anglers.

During the peak return of the Rearing Pond fish, the section of river from the Ponds downstream to the boat launch at the Wilson Access is the most heavily fished. Both boat and bank anglers flock to this section of river, and catch statistics reveal they have good cause.

This section of river is classic steelhead water with runs, flats, pockets, etc. All tactics will work when the fish are in, and all the typical tackle and techniques are used, including fly-fishing.

The Bogachiel, like many Olympic Peninsula rivers, also hosts runs of native fish. The later winter months (February, March and April) are the best times to fish the Bogey for these brutes and, needless to say, they should all be released unharmed.

Most anglers target these native steelhead in the upper river from the rearing ponds to the end of the road and beyond.

Trout

Although most anglers don't think of the Bogachiel as a trout stream, trout fishing in this river can be very good. Sea-run cutthroat enter midsummer and are available throughout the winter. Some anglers specifically target these anadromous cutthroat, but many are caught incidentally, by steelhead fishermen. Like sea-run cutthroat everywhere, look for these fish in the slower edge-water, pools, and around structure.

Fishing for resident trout can be very good in the upper Bogachiel. Hiking the Bogachiel River Trail provides immediate access to the river, but the consistent holding water starts after you've hiked in about eight miles. Trout fishing from this point upstream is the best. Persistent anglers have a shot at catching rainbow, cutthroat, eastern brook, whitefish, and Dolly Varden, as well as the anadromous species.

The Bogachiel has good trout fishing in addition to its steelhead.

The upper reaches of the Bogey are best suited to fly-fishing or other light tackle. The trout seem willing to take nearly any properly presented fly or small spinner tossed their way. This area has easy wading, and if you like remote fishing for trout that peak at around 12 inches in length, it's well worth the effort it takes to get there.

Floating the Bogachiel

Several boat ramps are located along the Bogachiel River (see map). The highest drift, from the ramp at the end of the South Bogachiel Road to Bogachiel State Park (about four miles) is the most difficult (Class II) and drifters should have experience and the capability to row around hazards.

The most popular drift is from the Rearing Pond Ramp down to the ramp at the Wilson Access. There are no real hazards in this stretch under normal flow conditions suited to angling, but drifters always need to be cognizant of the fact that new hazards can be born with each winter flood. One should always use caution, and be attentive when floating any coastal river.

Hiking and Other Activities

The Bogachiel River Trail leads deep into the Olympic Mountains. For several miles, the trail follows the river offering access to anglers, photographers, naturalists, and those simply after a hike in the woods. If you are looking for a more strenuous outing, the trail eventually terminates at its junction with the Mink Lake-Little Divide Trail twenty-three miles distant. This area offers a host of opportunities to the serious backpacker and mountain climber.

Bogachiel (Upper)

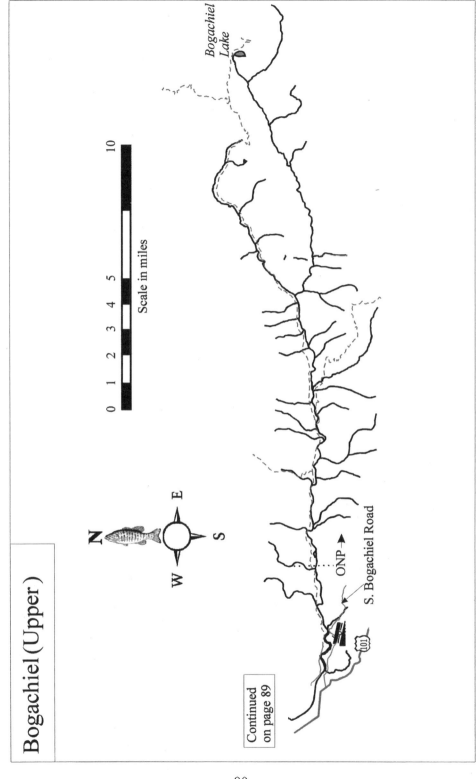

Scale in miles

Bogachiel Lake

ONP

S. Bogachiel Road

Continued on page 89

90

Bogachiel (Lower)

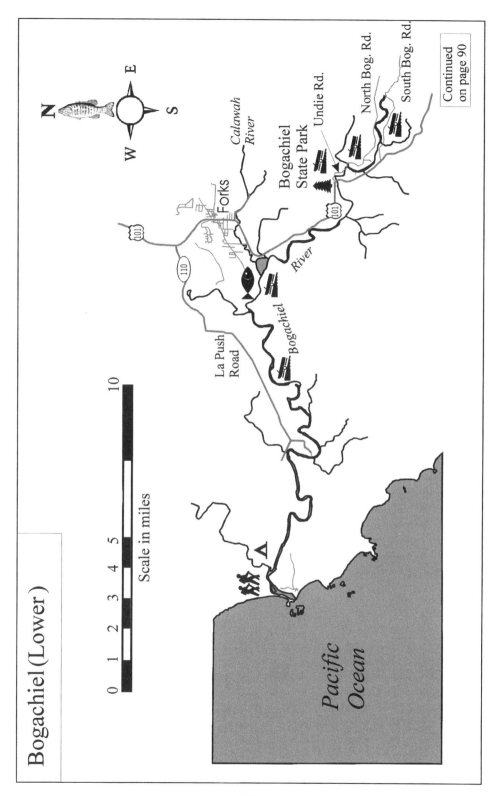

Scale in miles

0 1 2 3 4 5 10

N
W E
S

Calawah River

Forks

Bogachiel State Park

Undie Rd.

101

110

La Push Road

Bogachiel River

Pacific Ocean

North Bog. Rd.

South Bog. Rd.

Continued on page 90

Quillayute River

The Sol Duc and Bogachiel Rivers join to form the Quillayute River six miles from the Pacific Ocean. Both of these main forks are quite significant in their own right, and are joined by several other tributaries upstream. The most significant tributary is the Calawah River which joins the Bogachiel near the town of Forks. For the short distance that the Quillayute travels, it runs wide and fast.

Most of the visitors to this short river are there to fish. The Quillayute System, as this collective group of rivers is known, is one of the most productive in the state for the returning anadromous species. Summer and winter steelhead, spring and fall chinook, coho, chum, and sockeye salmon, as well as sea-run cutthroat trout, all make a strong showing in the Quillayute System. All must pass through the Quillayute to reach their natal streams.

Access to the Quillayute River is via the La Push Road, two miles north of Forks, which leads to the Mora Road, which parallels the Quillayute.

Fishing the Quillayute River

Even though all the anadromous species must travel up the Quillayute to reach their ultimate destinations, catching them in the big Quillayute is not as easy as it may seem. There is little holding water in the Quillayute, and fish most often make a beeline for the tributaries. This is not to say, however, that fish can't be taken; quite to the contrary, but anglers must use tactics suited to intercepting fish on the move.

Casting your arm off is the key to success for Quillayute fish. Since most anadromous fish are on the move, repeatedly pounding the water with cast after cast is one way to increase your chances. Reading the water and determining the most likely paths of travel is of paramount importance.

There are only a few spots along this short river offering bank access to anglers. Lyendecker Park, where the Sol Duc and Bogachiel merge to form the Quillayute, is a favorite. Here, bank anglers can fish the mouth of the Sol Duc and, although this is fast water, they do well intercepting fish headed upstream. Another point of access is downstream near the mouth at Mora Park.

The Sol Duc (right) and Bogachiel (left) join to form the Quillayute.

The Quillayute sees returning fish most of the season. Spring chinook overlap late winter steelhead in the early spring. Summer steelhead follow and overlap the fall runs of salmon, which are soon followed and overlapped by the winter runs of steelhead, which begin in November and continue throughout the winter and into the spring.

Floating the Quillayute River

Drifting the Quillayute is the most popular way to fish this river. Many floaters launch at one of the upstream ramps on the Bogachiel and float down to the ramp at Mora. For those wanting to drift only the Quillayute, the launch at Lyendecker Park is the start and the ramp at Mora Park is the exit, a distance of about five miles. Floating is straightforward, the only hazards being the occasional sweeper or log jam.

Quillayute

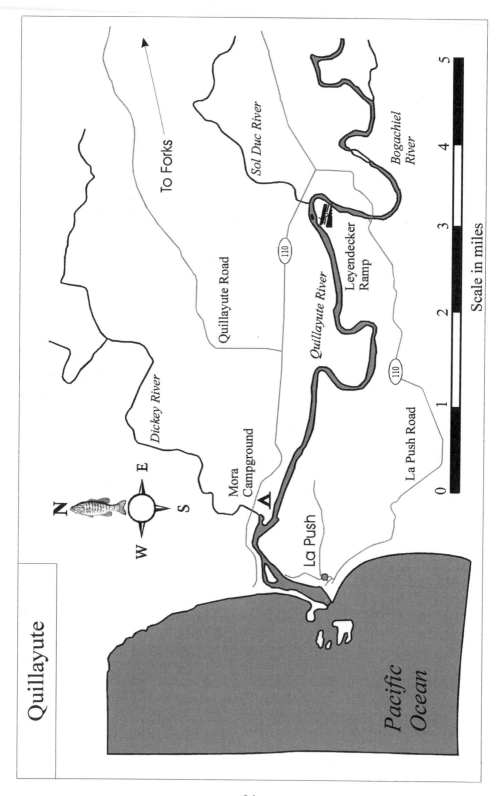

PART II

Strait of
Juan de Fuca
Streams

Winter on the Peninsula is beautiful and quiet.

Hoko River

Draining the hills in the northwest corner of the Olympic Peninsula, the Hoko River flows north and empties into the Strait of Juan De Fuca near the town of Sekiu. The Hoko is reached by taking State Route 112 two miles past Sekiu and turning left on the Hoko-Ozette Road. This road parallels much of the lower river providing good access to anglers.

The Hoko is a mid-sized river; easy to cast across and wade, therefore, easy to fish effectively. December and January are the months to be here, and when the water is right, the Hoko is a good producer of winter steelhead.

For fly-fishers, the Hoko is an especially worthy destination. From the upper Hoko Bridge to Ellis Creek Bridge (river mile 18.5), this river falls under fly-fishing only regulations. A gravel road provides access on the upper river.

Walking the upper Hoko you will see few other anglers. This river is pretty out of the way and doesn't receive as much pressure as many of the other peninsula rivers. Combined with the fly-fishing only regulations, the Hoko is a good bet for those seeking steelhead on the fly in a small stream situation.

The upper Hoko has well defined holes, riffles, and runs making it easy to identify holding lies. The rocky bottom makes for easy wading and, under optimum water conditions, one can work the water seldom leaving the streambed.

Sea-run cutthroat fishing can also be very good in the Hoko. These anadromous trout begin to show in September and are around through December.

Hoko

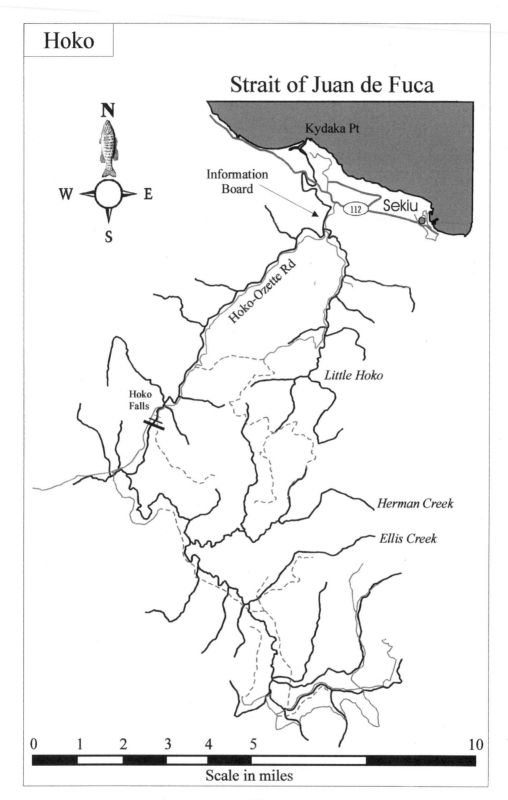

Strait of Juan de Fuca

Kydaka Pt

Information Board

112   Sekiu

Hoko-Ozette Rd

Little Hoko

Hoko Falls

Herman Creek

Ellis Creek

| 0 | 1 | 2 | 3 | 4 | 5 | 10 |

Scale in miles

Pysht River

The Pysht River is a small stream on the northern side of the Olympic Peninsula, reached by taking State Route 113 north of Sappho. The highway crosses the river after approximately nine miles. Just north of this crossing, State Route 112 connects, and follows the Pysht for much of its length before emptying into the Strait of Juan De Fuca.

Returns of planted steelhead are available during the winter, with December and January being the best months. This is small stream steelheading. Light tackle is what you need here, and since there is plenty of bushwhacking to be done while walking this stream, shorter rods are more practical than longer ones.

Fly-fishing little streams like the Pysht is a good way to go. It's easy to spot the holding water, and flies can be placed right on target as easily as with more conventional gear. The shallower water means that an unweighted fly line will often suffice.

The Pysht is a good choice when other streams are muddy or "blown" from too much rain. It takes a lot of precipitation to muddy this little stream, and if it does dirty, it clears fast.

During fall, the Pysht is a great sea-run cutthroat stream.

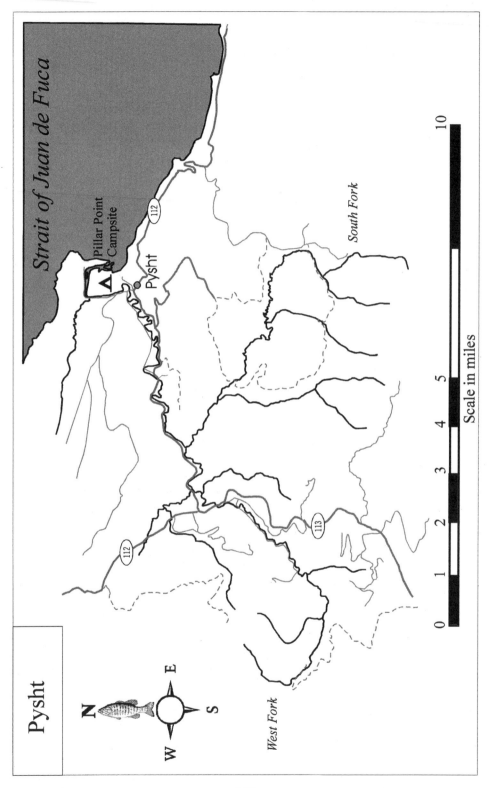

Pysht

Strait of Juan de Fuca

Pillar Point
Campsite

Pysht

112

112

113

West Fork

South Fork

N
W E
S

Scale in miles

0 1 2 3 4 5 10

100

Lyre River

The Lyre River is only five miles long. With its beginning at Lake Crescent, the Lyre flows north into the Strait of Juan De Fuca. Access is via trail, off State Route 112, about 18 miles west of Port Angeles.

Although there are a few summer steelhead that return to the Lyre, it is the run of winter steelhead that gets the attention of most anglers. The best time to fish this little stream is right after a rainstorm, as soon as the water clears, which doesn't take long. December and January are the best months for steelhead.

Sea-run cutthroat fishing can also be good during the fall. Cast to the usual places; pools, around structure and into any stagnant-looking water you can find.

One other interesting aspect of this watershed is the unique races of fish that inhabit Lake Crescent. A strain of rainbow trout known locally as the "Beardslee" and a special race of Lake Crescent cutthroat trout give a new dimension to the fishery.

Lyre

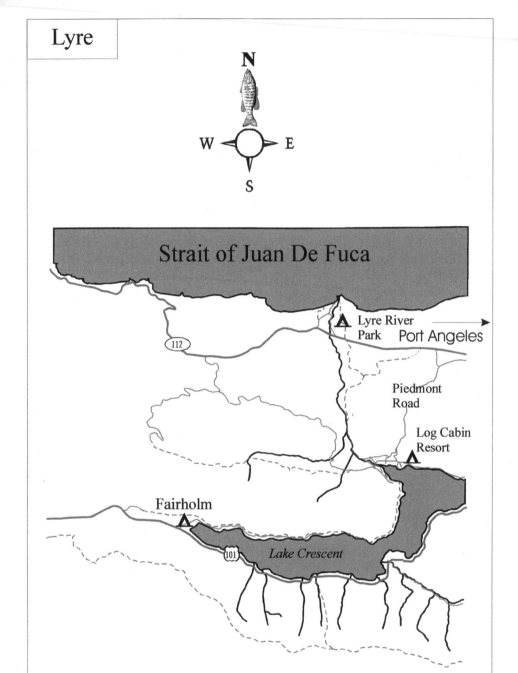

Strait of Juan De Fuca

112

Lyre River Park

Port Angeles →

Piedmont Road

Log Cabin Resort

Fairholm

101 Lake Crescent

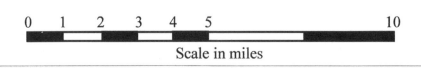

0   1   2   3   4   5   10

Scale in miles

Elwha River

The lower Elwha River is reached by taking U.S. 101 west from Port Angeles for roughly four miles until you reach State Route 112. Turn right and travel a couple more miles until you can turn right on the Elwha River Road. The upper river is reached via the Olympic Hot Springs Road off U.S. 101, eight miles from Port Angeles.

In the early 1900s, the Elwha and Glines Canyon Dams were built across the Elwha River, primarily for hydropower. Before the building of these dams the Elwha hosted tremendous runs of salmon. The most impressive were the chinook salmon, which grew to Kenai River proportions; 70, 90, and possibly even to 100 pounds.

When the dams were built, no consideration was given to anadromous fish passage, and as a consequence, this strain of giant chinook salmon, as well as the other anadromous runs, was forever erased. It is hard to imagine such nearsighted negligence.

In 1992 Congress approved the purchase of the dams with the intent of removing them. In 1998 the White House announced the allocation of $86 million for the removal of one of the two dams. The lower (Elwha) dam will be the first to go and the fate of the Glines Canyon Dam will depend on the successful return of anadromous fish after the removal of the lower dam.

Fishing the Elwha River

Although the great runs of chinook salmon are gone cannot be replaced by genetically inferior hatchery fish even if the dams are removed, the Elwha is still a good destination for anglers. Many species of fish are still seasonally found in the river below Elwha Dam including both summer and winter steelhead, coho and chinook salmon, rainbow, cutthroat and brook trout, sea-run cutthroat, Dolly Varden char and whitefish.

Steelhead

Summer steelheading on the lower Elwha produces a handful of fish for the persistent, but it is the winter run that surrenders most of the hatchery steelhead taken by those willing to put in the hours. Try fishing the brackish portions of the Elwha for fresh-from-the-salt fish. As is typical of hatchery-based runs, the winter fish are most available from December to February.

Salmon

Returns of hatchery coho in the lower Elwha provide some action for anglers in October. To a lesser extent, hatchery chinook also make an appearance.

Trout

It is the trout fishing found in the upper Elwha that deserves, and gets, most of the angling attention these days. Some of the best trout fishing in western Washington, and certainly the best trout fishing in the Olympics, is found in the upper reaches of this river.

The Elwha Road ends just beyond Lake Mills, and the Elwha River Trail begins. The best fishing is found above Mary's Falls, 8.7 miles from the trailhead. For the next several miles upstream, anglers willing to walk the distance can enjoy great angling for rainbow trout up to 20 inches, and some big Dolly Varden in the deeper holes.

Most anglers who venture this far up the Elwha camp at the Mary's Falls Camp and venture off from there. With certainty, if you are going to walk this far to fish, you should stay awhile and explore.

Selective Gear Rules are in effect on the Elwha. The upper river lends itself well to fly-fishing, and that's what most anglers do. Dry flies and nymphs produce well when presented appropriately. That's not to say that small spinners and spoons won't work also, but remember, single-barbless-hooks are the rule.

Lake Aldwell

Lake Aldwell is the 320 acre reservoir created by the Elwha Dam. Eastern brook, cutthroat, rainbow and kokanee can be found in this lake. Selective Gear Regulations are in effect here. The Elwha is fishable for several miles above Lake Aldwell, but fish populations are not as strong as those above Lake Mills. Still, one could fish in worse settings!

Lake Mills

Lake Mills is the 451 acre reservoir created by the Glines Canyon Dam. Rainbow, cutthroat, eastern brook, and Dolly Varden inhabit the lake. Fishing from a boat is the most practical way to fish this lake, but boaters should beware of sudden squalls when venturing out in small craft.

Hiking the Elwha River Valley

Besides the handful of energetic trout fishermen that hike into the upper Elwha, the Elwha River trail travels to the center of the Olympic Mountains, and is a very popular backpacking route.

From the Whiskey Bend Trailhead, the trail travels south along a hillside above the valley floor. The trail continues to climb away from the river and skirts the "Grand Canyon of the Elwha." At 8.7 miles from the trailhead, the trail descends to the river and a spur trail leads to the Mary's Falls Camp.

Another 1.9 miles upriver from the Mary's Falls Camp brings you to Canyon Camp, another popular destination for the angling hiker. The trail mostly follows the river now, and at mile 11.4 reaches the Elkhorn Ranger Station and Camp. At mile 16.7 a spur trail leads to the Hayes River Guard Station and Camp. The entire stretch of river from Mary's Falls to Hayes River is the prime trout water on the upper Elwha.

Lake Mills

Working up the valley, more camps are encountered, streams crossed, and breathtaking views of the Olympics are granted to hikers who make it this far. At mile 26.2, you arrive at Chicago Camp. Here the trail splits, and hikers have two options: 1) the Elwha Basin Trail, or 2) the Low Divide Trail.

The Elwha basin Trail continues on to Elwha Basin Camp at mile 29.0. This trail travels west from Chicago Camp. From the Elwha Basin Camp, climbers can access Dodwell-Rixon Pass.

The Low Divide Trail offers outstanding views of the Elwha Valley. At 28.6 miles, the trail comes to Lake Margaret and the junction with the North Fork Quinault Trail. At 31.2 miles you arrive at the Low Divide Camp. The Elwha trail and its branches provide a great destination or portal into the Olympic Mountains.

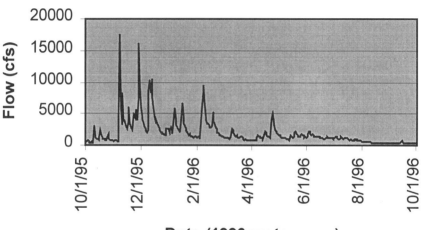

The Elwha River has some of the best trout fishing on the Peninsula.

The Pysht River.

The Duckabush River.

The Skokomish River.

Lake Constance.

The High Country, where all rivers begin.

Dungeness River

Draining the northeast corner of the Olympics, the Dungeness River empties into the Strait of Juan De Fuca near the town of Sequim. This was once a great salmon river, but recent years find the four species of Pacific salmon it hosts struggling.

The Dungeness is reached by taking U.S. 101 to Sequim. Sequim Avenue-Dungeness Way provides access to the lower river. The upper stretches can be reached by taking Palo Alto Road, off U.S. 101, to Forest Road 2860, which eventually gets you to the Upper Dungeness Trailhead. There are a couple campgrounds along the way named Dungeness Forks and East Crossing.

Fishing the Dungeness

The Dungeness hosts both summer and winter steelhead. Summer steelheading is only open during the month of June to protect the run of pink salmon, and only a handful of summer fish are taken. Winter steelhead fishing is more productive, and during the course of the winter season, those who frequent the river catch a few hundred fish. If hooked, all salmon except for coho (check the current regulations for seasons and closures) must be released. Trout fishing on the Dungeness (except for sea-run cutthroat) is best above the confluence with the Gray Wolf River. Access is available around the Dungeness Forks Campground. The next good access point is near the East Crossing Campground. The Lower Dungeness Trail provides several miles of good angling access. From the parking lot at the end of the road, the Upper Dungeness Trail will lead anglers to the river (now a small stream) in many places. Rainbow trout and Dolly Varden char will be the catch in the Dungeness. Don't expect monster trout; a 12 incher is a whopper. The occasional Dolly to 15 inches can also be found in the upper stretches of this river.

Hiking the Upper Dungeness Trail

This is a 9.7-mile backpack trek through the Buckhorn Wilderness, offering great views of the northern Olympic Mountains. Eventually the trail leads to Home Lake, within the National Park boundary. At the lake the route becomes the Constance Pass Trail, providing access to several peaks for mountain climbers. If you cross the divide, you will drop down into the Dosewallips Valley.

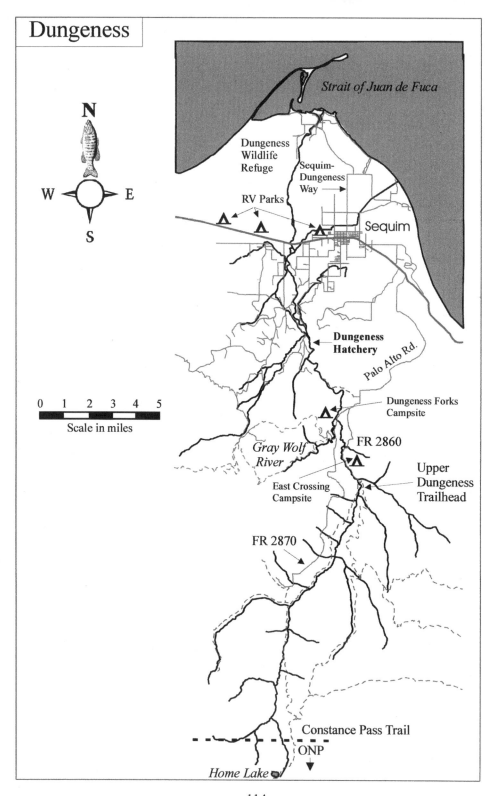

Dungeness

Strait of Juan de Fuca

Dungeness
Wildlife
Refuge

Sequim-
Dungeness
Way

RV Parks

Sequim

**Dungeness
Hatchery**

Palo Alto Rd.

Dungeness Forks
Campsite

**Gray Wolf
River**

FR 2860

East Crossing
Campsite

Upper
Dungeness
Trailhead

FR 2870

Constance Pass Trail

ONP

Home Lake

N
W E
S

0 1 2 3 4 5
Scale in miles

Part III

Hood Canal / Puget Sound Streams

Hamma Hamma River.

Dosewallips River

The Dosewallips River is the northernmost of the eastern Olympic streams that drains into Hood Canal. It is generally thought of as the Lower Dosewallips from the mouth upstream to Dosewallips Falls, 13.7 miles distant. The Upper Dosewallips is the section of stream above the falls.

Access is via the Dosewallips Road, off U.S. 101. This road parallels the river for several miles. Much of the lower river runs through private property and access is poor. The further upstream you get, the more access improves. Above the falls there is a mile of road providing fishing access, then anglers must take to the trail which follows the mainstream all the way to its headwaters near Hayden Pass. There are no official boat ramps on the river and the falls are not safe for boating.

The river runs cloudy most of the season due to glacial runoff from Silt Creek, which joins the mainstem inside the National Park boundary. It is only during the late summer that the upper river clears enough to fish for trout.

Fishing the Dosewallips

Anadromous Fish

There are only a handful of winter steelhead that return to this river each year. Anglers who hook one are lucky indeed. Chum salmon make an appearance in November and December, and they provide the bulk of the anadromous fish action in the lower river. Sea-run cutthroat appear in the fall and can provide good fishing for those targeting them. A good point of access when seeking the anadromous species is Dosewallips State Park, right at U.S. 101.

Trout

Like the other rivers draining the eastern Olympics, trout are the real prize for anglers. Good trout water can be found from Dosewallips Falls upstream for several miles. Elkhorn Campground and Dosewallips Campground, both on the upper river, provide good access for camping anglers.

As with most Olympic Peninsula rivers, the trout found in the Dosewallips are not going to be monsters. Rainbows in the 8-12 inch range are what you can expect, with the average size dropping the further upstream you go.

From the end of the road, the Dosewallips River trail follows the stream for several miles. There are several points along the way where you can hike down to the river and gain fishing access. A couple miles in, the West Fork joins the main Dosewallips. The West Fork runs clean and is likely to provide plenty of small rainbows. About five miles up the mainstream, you come to Silt Creek. Above this murky tributary, the mainstem is clear and holds small rainbow, cutthroat, and eastern brook trout.

The Dosewallips River Trail

This trail provides access to many hiking and climbing routes in the eastern Olympic Mountains. The trail begins at the end of the Dosewallips Road, behind the Ranger Station. The trail roughly follows the river valley for its entire length.

The Anderson Pass Trail spurs off after 1.4 miles, roughly following the West Fork of the Dosewallips. The Constance Pass Trail is reached at mile 2.5. Hiking it will take you north into the Dungeness watershed. At mile 9.3, the Gray Wolf Trail spurs off. It also travels north to the Gray Wolf River, a major tributary of the Dungeness. At mile 12.7, the Dose Meadows camping area, and junctions with Hayden Pass and the Cameron Pass trail, are reached. This trail is a major corridor for backcountry travel and high routes.

Dosewallips River.

Dosewallips (Upper)

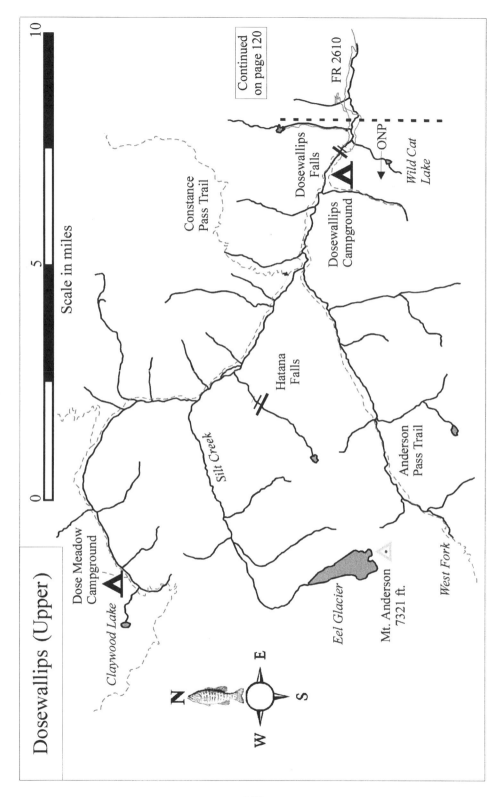

Scale in miles

Continued on page 120

FR 2610

Dosewallips Falls

ONP

Wild Cat Lake

Dosewallips Campground

Constance Pass Trail

Hatana Falls

Silt Creek

Anderson Pass Trail

Dose Meadow Campground

Claywood Lake

Eel Glacier

Mt. Anderson 7321 ft.

West Fork

N
W   E
S

119

Dosewallips (Lower)

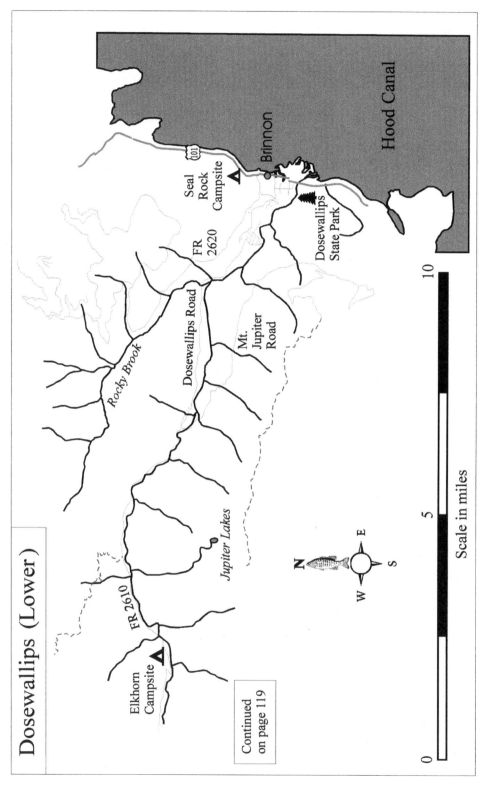

Hood Canal

Brinnon

Seal Rock Campsite

Dosewallips State Park

FR 2620

Dosewallips Road

Rocky Brook

Mt. Jupiter Road

Jupiter Lakes

FR 2610

Elkhorn Campsite

Continued on page 119

N
W E
S

Scale in miles

0   5   10

Duckabush River

Access to the Duckabush River is via the Duckabush Road off U.S. 101. The road travels 6.5 miles from U.S. 101 to its end. Here a trail begins and follows the river for several miles.

Fishing the Duckabush

The Duckabush hosts winter and summer steelhead, chum salmon, sea-run cutthroat and rainbow trout. Only a handful of steelhead are caught each season. Chum salmon fishing can be good in November and December, but since most of the lower river flows through private property, access is poor. Hitting the river from Collins campground gives the angler the best access on the lower river.

Sea-run cutthroat fishing is fair in the fall. Resident rainbow fishing for smallish trout is possible all along the upper Duckabush. Walking the river trail you will find access trails leading down to the water.

The Duckabush River Trail

The Duckabush River Trail is a 21.1 mile trek from Forest Road 2510 to Marmot Lake. A pair of "humps" (Big and Little) add significant topography to the hike, but access to the river is frequent if you're willing to whack a bit of brush. The upper Duckabush is very scenic, and gets plenty of attention from hikers. At the end of the trail, Marmot Lakes, Hart Lake and La Crosse Lake can be accessed. The end this trail connects to O'Neal Pass where you can exit through either the Quinault, Dosewallips, or Skokomish watersheds.

Chum salmon enter the lower Duckabush, but shore access is difficult.

Duckabush (Upper)

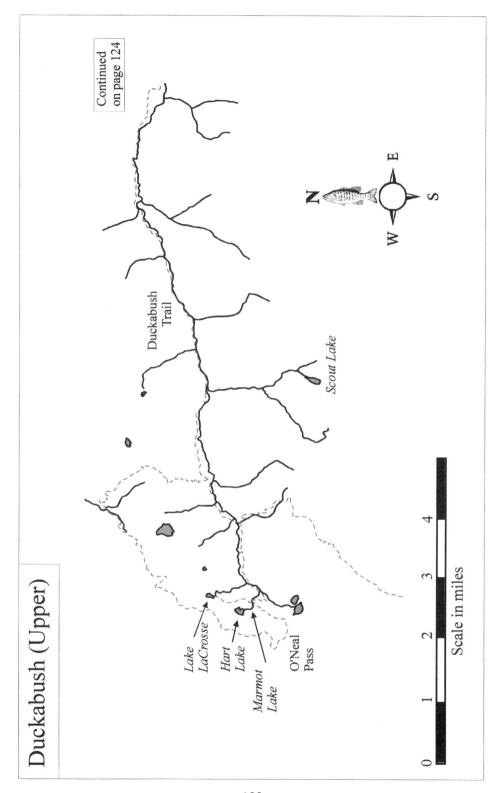

Continued on page 124

Duckabush Trail

Scout Lake

Lake LaCrosse

Hart Lake

Marmot Lake

O'Neal Pass

N
E
W
S

0   1   2   3   4

Scale in miles

123

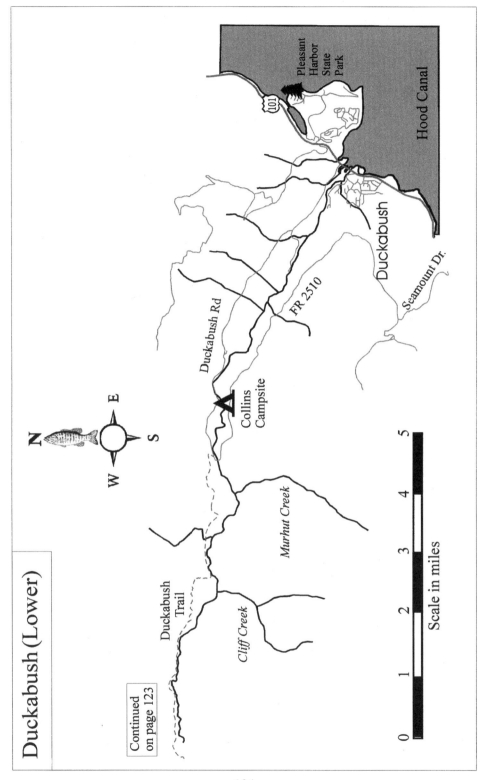

Duckabush (Lower)

Continued on page 123

Scale in miles

0 1 2 3 4 5

N
W E
S

Duckabush Trail

Cliff Creek

Murhut Creek

Collins Campsite

Duckabush Rd

FR 2510

Duckabush

Seamount Dr.

101

Pleasant Harbor State Park

Hood Canal

Hamma Hamma River

About four miles up the Hamma Hamma a spectacular falls abruptly ends the migration of anadromous fish in this eastern Olympics River, which drains into Hood Canal. Limited access to the lower river is off Highway 101 near the highway bridge. The upper river is reached by taking the Hamma Hamma Road (FR 25) or the Jorstad Creek Road (FR 24).

The upper Hamma Hamma is one of the prettiest rivers draining the eastern Olympics. The water is crystal clear and screams out... fish me!

Fishing the Hamma Hamma

There is a small run of steelhead and salmon returning to the lower Hamma Hamma each season. Finding a place to fish for them in the short stretch of river is difficult. Access to the river is all through private property.

If you do obtain permission to fish the lower river, it is the sea-run cutthroat that will be the most abundant during the fall. Casting wet flies or small spinners are sure to work if the fish are around.

Where the Hamma Hamma really shines is for its trout fishing. The best trout fishing is found along the Jorstad Creek Road, from Lena Creek downstream. Rainbow trout are planted here and can be taken along with resident cutthroat.

The section of river above Lena Creek is much smaller, and although difficult to fish, holds larger trout. A short fly rod, a box full of dry flies, a warm summer day, and plenty of patience can pay off here.

There is a U.S Forest Service campground on the north bank of the river near the fishing action.

Hamma Hamma

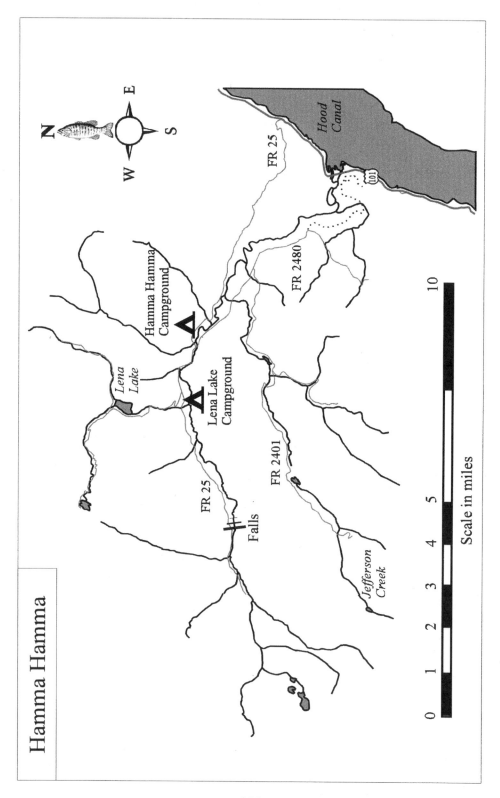

Scale in miles

Skokomish River

Draining the southeastern Olympic Mountains, the Skokomish watershed is comprised mainly of two streams–the North and South Forks of the Skokomish River. The rivers join not too far from the southern end of Hood Canal, into which they spill.

The South Fork Skokomish is reached by turning left off U.S. 101 onto the Skokomish Valley Road, which leads to Brown Creek Campground, 17 miles distant. Above the campground the Lower South Fork Trail begins.

The North Fork Skokomish is reached by taking the Lake Cushman Road off U.S. 101 and following it to the Staircase Ranger Station and campground, just past the end of the lake. Here the North Fork Skokomish River Trail begins.

Skokomish River.

Fishing the Skokomish

Like many rivers of the northwest, the Skokomish was once a great steelhead and salmon stream. Man has traditionally had a way of screwing things up, of course, all in the name of progress. The North Fork Skokomish is dammed in two places forming Cushman and Kokanee lakes.

This changes the entire ecosystem, usually for the worse, especially if you happen to be an anadromous fish. We now live with the results of our actions. Changes such as flow modification, fish ladders and even dam removal to allow fish passage and restore natural flow regimes are expensive, but actively being considered.

Steelhead Fishing

Today, the mainstream of the "Skoke" only sees a modest number of steelhead return each season, but you can fish for them in the lower reaches, reached via the Skokomish Valley Road.

Although thousands of winter steelhead smolts are planted each season, only a handful return. This fact only strengthens the argument that nature knows best. Hatcheries and planted fish cannot replace a fishery destroyed by thoughtless alteration of a river.

If you catch steelhead on the Skoke, consider yourself lucky, and by all means...release it.

Salmon Fishing

Chum salmon are an attraction during late fall, and the lower river produces well some years for both gear and fly-fishers for this catch-and-release salmon fishery.

Willing to take just about anything offered (especially if it is chartreuse), this aggressive salmon gets much attention in the lower river.

Trout Fishing

Trout are the major attraction on the Skokomish. Both the South and North Forks hold trout, but it is the North Fork that produces best.

South Fork Skokomish

The trail along the South Fork begins above Brown Creek Campground. The river in this immediate area gets a lot of pressure and is not real productive. There is a canyon, which extends about a mile upstream from the campground, and it is above this canyon where the best trout fishing can be found. Rainbows, reaching 18 inches or so, are taken from these waters. As you travel upstream, cutthroat predominate, although they are usually much smaller.

North Fork Skokomish

Nearly all of the North Fork Skokomish flows within the boundaries of Olympic National Park. Under catch-and-release regulations, the North Fork is truly a stream to cherish.

At certain times, the river just above the lake (before Staircase Rapids), hosts Dolly Varden, kokanee, Cushman chinook salmon, rainbow and cutthroat trout. During spawning season though, the river here is closed to fishing to ensure adequate reproduction.

Above the Staircase Rapids the river mellows a bit and is excellent for casting flies to rainbow and cutthroat trout, with rainbows being the predominate species. The river is fishable and productive for several miles upstream.

As with most mountain-type streams, try small dry flies. Adams, Elk Hair Caddis, Royal Coachmans and Humpys work well. The North Fork is less affected by glacial runoff than many other Olympic streams which has two main effects. First, the stream runs extremely clear, so long, light, tippets are the rule. Second, the flow comes sooner in the year, and fishing is often good starting in June.

This is a stream built for rock-hopping, short casts, and using streamside vegetation to break up your silhouette. Stalking your prey will ultimately pay off in this sparkling little stream.

Fishing Lake Cushman

This large reservoir holds rainbow and cutthroat trout, kokanee, landlocked chinook salmon, and bull trout. The best fishing seems to be on the upper end of the lake near the inlet and along the stream bed of the buried North Fork of the Skokomish. Gear anglers do the best here, and timing is paramount to intercept fish staging to make their spawning run up the North Fork.

There are three boat ramps on the east side of the lake. A Department of Fish and Wildlife ramp located near the south end, one at Lake Cushman Resort, and one at Lake Cushman State Park.

Other Activities

Both the North Fork and South Fork Skokomish Rivers host trail systems leading deep into the Olympics. Although the trail leading up the South Fork is less elaborate than the North Fork Trail, it still travels along the river for approximately 9 miles. The trail becomes progressively more faint as it crosses Sundown Pass and joins the Lake Sundown route.

The North Fork Skokomish Trail starts at the Staircase Ranger Station. The trail roughly follows the river for nine miles to Nine Stream Camp (9.2 miles) and eventually climbs to its junction with the Duckabush River Trail at 15.1 miles.

Notable spur trails include Flapjack Lakes trail at 3.5 miles (also climbing access to Mt. Cruiser), and the Black and White Lakes spur trail at 5.3 miles.

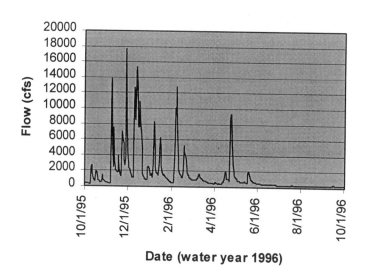

Skokomish River Flow
Station 1231033 near Potlatch

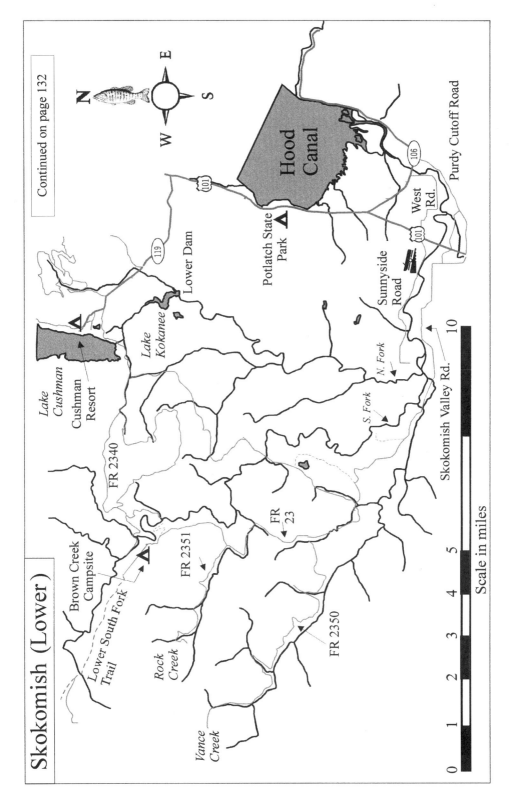

Skokomish (Lower)

Continued on page 132

N
W E
S

Hood Canal

Potlatch State Park ▲

Lake Cushman
Cushman Resort ▲

Lake Kokanee

Lower Dam

119

101

106

West Rd.

Purdy Cutoff Road

Sunnyside Road

N. Fork

S. Fork

Skokomish Valley Rd.

FR 2340

FR 2351

FR 23

FR 2350

Brown Creek Campsite ▲

Lower South Fork Trail

Rock Creek

Vance Creek

Scale in miles
0 1 2 3 4 5 10

131

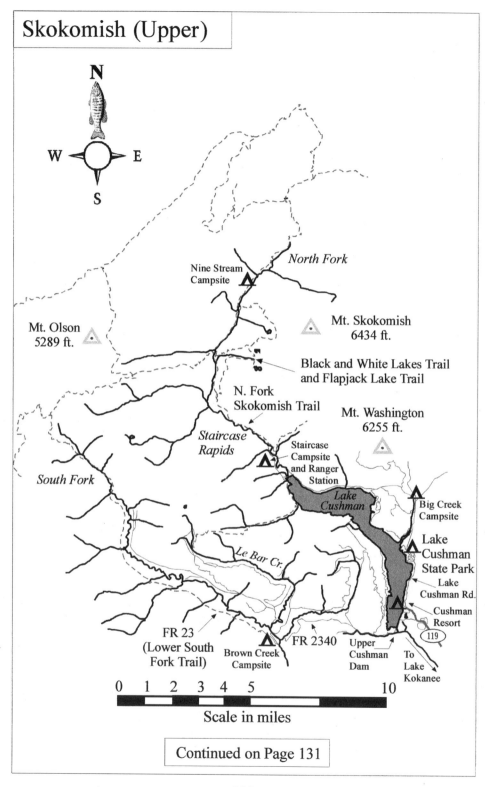

Skokomish (Upper)

N
W   E
S

Nine Stream Campsite

North Fork

Mt. Olson 5289 ft.

Mt. Skokomish 6434 ft.

Black and White Lakes Trail and Flapjack Lake Trail

N. Fork Skokomish Trail

Mt. Washington 6255 ft.

Staircase Rapids

Staircase Campsite and Ranger Station

Lake Cushman

Big Creek Campsite

South Fork

Lake Cushman State Park

Le Bar Cr.

Lake Cushman Rd.

Cushman Resort

119

FR 23 (Lower South Fork Trail)

Brown Creek Campsite

FR 2340

Upper Cushman Dam

To Lake Kokanee

0   1   2   3   4   5   10

Scale in miles

Continued on Page 131

The High Country

If you venture up the rivers of the Olympic Peninsula to their headwaters – beyond the small tributaries and feeder streams, into the sub-alpine and alpine regions, you will find, in most watersheds, lakes. Many of the lakes found in the high country host trout. All of the high lakes are surrounded by beauty unimaginable by those who have never ventured so far into the backcountry.

The rewards of hiking into the high country are many, but it is the beautiful trout lakes that keep me trekking the often-soggy miles through the rain forest, past the montane zone and into the sub-alpine and alpine regions where such lakes are found.

You will not find monster trout here. If length and girth are your quest, you will be happier fishing the rivers in the valleys for the anadromous species. Trout of the high country will mostly be under a foot long; a 15-incher is a prize indeed.

Although not monsters, the trout found in the lakes of the high country are wild. Many years ago the National Park Service stopped planting these lakes in favor of natural propagation. Their goal was to preserve the Park as a natural ecosystem. Although I enjoy pursuing fish in these pristine lakes, introducing them where they did not previously exist can disrupt the balance of other species such as native amphibians. As a result, a few of the smaller lakes not conducive to natural spawning are barren of trout.

Long before the National Park Service stopped planting trout within its boundaries, eastern brook trout were planted in many of the high lakes. They did well, and are now the predominant species of the high country. Rainbow and cutthroat trout can be found in lakes with good stream influx, although there are only a few of these inside the National Park boundary.

Outside the Park boundary, the State of Washington continues to stock the lakes of the Olympic Mountains. Some of these stockings fail for various reasons but the trout in many lakes thrive. An example of the latter is Price's Lake near Lake Cushman. Here anglers can expect to catch rainbow, cutthroat, and brook trout up to 20 inches.

Fishing the High Country

Winter snow pack determines when many of the high country lakes open. The lower lakes are often ice-free by the general opener – the last weekend in April. However, many of the higher lakes won't ice-off until mid-July to late August. When the ice does free, trout will be feeding on nearly any food item that comes their way.

The best places to concentrate your fishing will be around and over weedbeds, along structure, and at the mouths of streams either entering or leaving the lake. Cloudy days will produce the best (not usually a problem in the Olympics), or early morning and late evening when the most insect activity commonly takes place.

Gear

Light tackle is all you need in the high country. For fly rods a 4-weight to 5-weight is adequate. The most difficult task is always reaching the fish. For this reason, many anglers take lightweight spinning rods and casting bubbles. A casting bubble is a plastic device (filled with water) attached to your main line. A four or five foot section of 4X or 5X tippet is then connected, along with your fly, at the end. This setup will allow you to cast quite a distance and is perhaps the best way to cover a small lake if you are a shore-bound angler.

If you can afford the weight, a lightweight inflatable float tube or personal boat should be considered. Some of the new products on the market fold down to just a few pounds, are easy to inflate with small foot pumps, and will give you the mobility needed to cover even the larger high country lakes.

One does not need piles of gear when fishing these lakes. Your rod and reel, a few tippets, fly floatant, insect repellent and a handful of flies are all you really need, but you can add to suit personal wants or needs. Simplicity is one of the virtues of this kind of experience. As for flies, a simple collection in sizes 16 to 12 is adequate. My personal high country box includes the Adams, elk-hair caddis, Royal Coachman, mosquito, black midge, chironomid pupa, hare's-ear nymph, pheasant-tail nymph, freshwater scud and the woolly bugger.

Reaching the High Country

As you have read throughout this guide, trail systems extend up most of the river systems to the high country. Locating the trout lakes can be done by obtaining any number of maps; the one given to you when entering the Olympic National Park, *DeLorme's Atlas & Gazetteer*, USGS topographic maps, or maps included in Olympic hiking guides.

If traveling into the high country to fish, make sure you check with the Olympic National Park (360) 452-0330 for current regulations.

Final Thoughts

The Pacific Northwest is blessed to have such a beautiful and wild place as the Olympic Peninsula. We were all fortunate when President Roosevelt signed the bill establishing Olympic National Park. Besides the network of hiking trails (500 miles of formal trails), the area within the Park remains much as it has always been.

With the ever-increasing population, more and more people are venturing into the backcountry. We must all do our part to insure our presence makes as little impact on the land and water as possible. Do your best to leave no trace when hiking, camping, floating, or fishing.

The excellent fishing in most rivers of the Olympic Peninsula is still available to everyone. More anglers, however, inevitably have an impact on the fishery. If the great fishing is to continue, minimal and no kill policies should be adopted on most waters. As of this writing, the Washington Department of Fish and Wildlife still allows the killing of wild steelhead on many Olympic Peninsula rivers. This is a blatant disregard for the resource. Despite what state officials might allow, the wise thing to do is release all wild steelhead unharmed. Ideally, this also means single barbless hooks and no bait to reduce accidental mortality.

History shows us over and over again how the greed and carelessness of man negatively impacts our planet. We must all do our part to protect the magnificent Olympic Peninsula if we want its mountains, rain forests, lakes, rivers, and abundant life to remain pristine for generations to come. If we don't, all will be lost. I guarantee it.

Mount Olympus

Elwha River, 7, 106, 107, 108, 109
Enchanted Valley, 37, 39

G

Glacier Creek, 62
Glacier Meadows Campground, 62
Glines Canyon Dam, 107, 108
Grand Canyon of the Elwha, 109
Gray Wolf River, 113, 116

H

Hamma Hamma River, 8, 114, 124
Hartzell, 50, 51
Hayden Pass, 115, 116
Hayes River, 109
High Divide Loop Tail, 77
Hoh Rainforest Visitors Center, 62
Hoh River, 7, 53, 56, 57, 59, 62, 63, 77
Hoko River, 7, 97
Hood Canal, 8, 113, 115, 124, 126
Huelsdonk, John, 56
Humptulips River, 7, 27

J

Juan de Fuca, 11, 95

K

Klahowya State Park, 70

L

Lake Aldwell, 108
Lake Crescent, 103
Lake Cushman, 126, 129, 133
Lake Cushman State Park., 129
Lake Margaret, 111
Lake Mills, 108, 109
Lake Quinault, 33, 38
Lake Wynoochee, 16, 20
Lyendecker Park, 92, 93
Lyman rapids, 46, 50
Lyre River, 7, 103

M

Marmot Lake, 121
Mary's Falls, 108, 109

Mora Park, 92, 93
Morgan's Crossing, 57, 61
Mt. Olympus, 9, 12, 44, 53, 62, 77
Mt. Queets, 44

N

National Park Service, 49, 62, 133
Nolan Bar, 57, 58, 61

O

O'Neal Pass, 121
Olympic Mountains, 9, 12, 13, 43, 44, 56, 67, 85, 88, 109, 111, 114, 116, 126, 133, 137
Olympic National Park, 11, 13, 34, 39, 45, 57, 129, 134, 135, 136, 137
O'Neil, Joseph P., 11, 44
Oxbow, 61

P

Price's Lake, 133
Pysht River, 100

Q

Queets Campground, 45, 48, 50, 52, 54
Queets River, 7, 41, 42, 43, 44, 51, 53, 54
Quillayute River, 7, 65, 67, 83, 91, 93
Quinault Indian Reservation, 34, 41, 45, 51
Quinault River, 7, 33, 35, 39, 53

R

rainbow trout. *See* trout, rainbow

S

salmon
    chinook, 18, 24, 28, 41, 45, 48, 57, 59, 65, 67, 69, 86, 91, 93, 106, 107, 129
    chum, 18, 24, 28, 67, 91, 115, 120, 121
    chun, 128
    coho, 18, 24, 28, 41, 45, 57, 60, 65, 67, 69, 83, 91, 107, 113
    pink, 113
Salmon River, 45, 46, 50
Sam's rapids, 46, 50
Sappho, 100
Satsop River, 7, 23, 24
Schafer State Park, 23, 25
Sea-run cutthroat. *See* trout, cutthroat
Sekiu, 97
Selective Gear Regulations, 82, 108

Skokomish River, 8, 126, 127
Sol Duc Campground, 77
Sol Duc Falls, 77, 78
Sol Duc Hot Springs, 77
Sol Duc River, 7, 67
steelhead
    summer, 18, 28, 45, 47, 48, 59, 67, 69, 82, 93, 103, 120
    winter, 18, 28, 37, 41, 45, 47, 57, 58, 67, 68, 82, 86, 91, 93, 97, 103, 107, 113, 115, 128
Stevens Creek, 27
Strait of Juan de Fuca, 7, 9
Strait of Juan De Fuca, 97, 100, 103, 113
Streaters Crossing, 50, 51

T

Taholah, 33
Tom Creek, 57
trout
    cutthroat, 25, 28, 29, 38, 41, 45, 49, 57, 60, 65, 67, 69, 70, 86, 87, 91, 98, 101, 103, 104,
        107, 108, 113, 115, 116, 120, 121, 124, 125, 129, 133
    rainbow, 37, 87, 103, 104, 107, 108, 113, 116, 120, 121, 125, 128, 129, 133
Tshletshy Creek, 53

W

whitefish, 37, 38, 63, 87, 107
Wynoochee Falls, 16
Wynoochee River, 7, 16, 18

Other Books Available from Ecopress:

The James River Guide (Virginia) – coming in early 2000
The Susquehanna River Guide (Pennsylvania / Maryland) – 120 pages, $11.95
Floating and Recreation on Montana's Rivers – 370 pages, $17.95
The Trinity Alps Companion (California) – 254 pages, $14.95
Two Wheels Around New Zealand – 286 pages, $12.95
Native Conifers of the Pacific Northwest – trifold laminated card for outdoors, $4.95
Reconnecting With Nature – 230 pages, $14.95

Call 1-800-326-9272 or visit our website at www.ecopress.com and get 10% off!

Olympic Peninsula Rivers

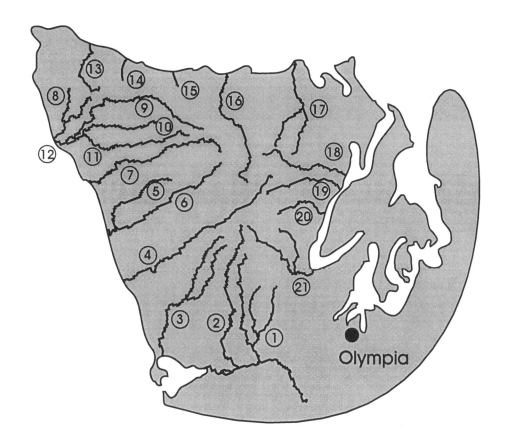

1) Satsop River - page 21
2) Wynoochee River - page 21
3) Humptulips River - page 25
4) Quinault River - page 31
5) Clearwater River - page 41
6) Queets River - page 43
7) Hoh River - page 55
8) Dickey River - page 63
9) Sol Duc River - page 65
10) Calawah River - page 81
11) Bogachiel River - page 85

12) Quillayute River - page 91
13) Hoko River - page 97
14) Pysht River - page 99
15) Lyre River - page 101
16) Elwha River - page 103
17) Dungeness - page 113
18) Dosewallips River - page 117
19) Duckabush River - page 121
20) Hamma Hamma River - page 125
21) Skokomish River - page 127

141

River Notes :

River Notes :